C000231484

Wales Before 1066

Prehistoric and Celtic Wales:
facing the Romans, Saxons and the Vikings

Donald Gregory

Gwasg Carreg Gwalch

First published in 1989; new edition: 2018
© text: Donald Gregory estate
Cover image and images inside © Crown copyright
(2016) Visit Wales
© publication: Gwasg Carreg Gwalch 2018

ISBN: 978-1-84524-210-7
Cover design: Eleri Owen
Published by Gwasg Carreg Gwalch,
12 Iard yr Orsaf, Llanrwst, Wales LL26 0EH
tel: 01492 642031
email: llanrwst@carreg-gwalch.cymru
website: www.carreg-gwalch.cymru

Acknowledgements

The publishers are grateful to the family of the deceased author for every co-operation in launching this new edition.

Donald Gregory (1911 – 2006) became a Radnor youth when his father became postmaster at Llandrindod. He became familiar with the remote countryside of moors and hills and interested in its past and heritage. Later, as a history student and teacher, his obsession with understanding and appreciating the past evolved to cover the whole of Wales. He and his wife spent decades of their holidays on the bylanes of Wales, visiting the places where history comes alive.

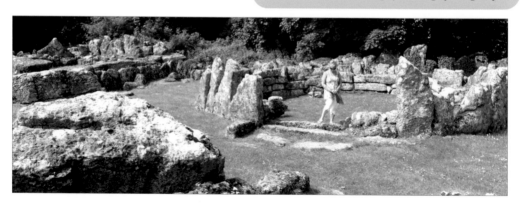

Celtic dwelling of Dinllugwy, Anglesey

Contents

Introduction

In 1536 the Act of Union was heralded in London as the union of England and Wales, whereby the two countries were to become one, the age-old differences in race, culture and history expected miraculously to fuse together in the parliamentary crucible. Four hundred and fifty years later, however, these differences remained. Devolution in 1997 brought its own government to Wales, as England's first colony once again faced a future of self-determination, embracing its responsibilities to its people, its culture and its past.

To many English people, the real history of England began with the Norman conquest. All that went before is regarded as an interesting collection of stories about prehistoric man, the Celts and the Romans, the Saxons and the Danes, which together provide a picturesque introduction to the main narrative. The people of Wales, on the other hand, tend not to look at their past in this way at all; to start with, very many Welshmen have ancestors who lived in Britain long before the arrival in these islands of the forebears

of most contemporary English people. It has to be remembered, too, that the Welsh have not always been mostly confined to the hills in the west: circumstances, as will be shown, drove them further and further back into the hills until some sort of a line of demarcation between Wales and England was established in the eighth century by the Mercian king, Offa.

Early settlers in these islands though the Welsh were, they were by no means the first to live in what we now call Wales. Something will be said of their predecessors when the prehistory of the country is under consideration. Suffice is to say here that the Celts, who were the ancestors of those who today live in Ireland, the Highlands of Scotland, the Isle of Man, Cornwall, Brittany and Wales, crossed the sea into these islands in about 500 BC, their arrival being thought to mark the end of the Bronze and the beginning of the Iron Age. It was originally believed that the Continental Celts crossed the Channel from northern France but later archaeological discoveries favour the western ocean route from southern and western Europe to the western shores of Cornwall and Wales. When in the first century AD, 500 years later, the Romans invaded Britain, they found that these Celts were firmly established in the hilly country in the west. There, roused by their druidical religious leaders, with whom the Romans had already clashed in Gaul, they presented a fierce challenge to the invaders. The animated crowds of rugby supporters who every other year cross the Dee, the Severn and the Wye to shout encouragement to their fellow-countrymen at Twickenham, are the proud representatives of a sturdily independent, unassimilated and radically different racial group from the English.

Iron Age hut near Holyhead

Prehistoric Times

The earliest inhabitants

Northern Europe in its prehistory was several times covered with vast sheets of ice; in the intervals between these ice ages there were long interglacial periods, when life abounded. Enough evidence has accumulated in recent years to prove that early men sometimes took shelter during these interglacial periods in the limestone caves to be found in the Clwyd valley. No skeleton has survived but enough human bones have come to light to enable archaeologists to determine, thanks to the wonders of radiocarbon dating methods, just when the human occupation of these caves took place. The date agreed is c. 180,000 BC. The ice subsequently returned and human life disappeared from the valley, only to return once again when the next interglacial period made human occupation possible in other limestone caves in the same valley. This later occupation has been carbon-dated as c. 50,000 BC.

In the last Ice Age, which ended somewhere between 10,000 and 9,000 BC, ice covered the whole of Wales except for the most south-westerly parts and Gower (Gŵyr). In a cave in the parish of Paviland in the south-western corner of the peninsula, south-east of Worms Head, an early archaeologist from Oxford, William Buckland, in 1823 discovered a human skeleton which had been buried along with ivory implements and the bones of a mammoth. Some ritual was believed to have accompanied the interment, as the skeleton, which was found in a standing position against the wall of the cave, was stained red. The excited Dean had the precious find taken to Oxford, where it acquired the interesting name of 'The Red Lady of Paviland'. Archaeologists today have more sophisticated tools at their disposal; in consequence it is now known that the skeleton, which had been stained red by the iron oxide in the soil, was of a young man of about twenty-five years old. Furthermore, carbon-dating proved that the young man died in about 16,500 BC, some 10,000 years after the death of the mammoth found with him.

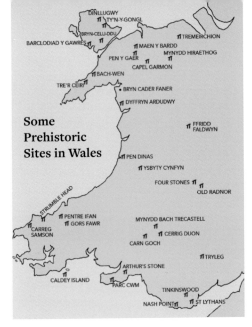

Some Prehistoric Sites in Wales

DINLLUGWY
TY'N-Y-GONGL
BRYN-CELLI-DDU
TREMEIRCHION
BARCLODIAD Y GAWRES
MAEN Y BARDD
MYNYDD HIRAETHOG
PEN Y GAER
CAPEL GARMON
BACH-WEN
TRE'R CEIRI
BRYN CADER FANER
DYFFRYN ARDUDWY
FFRIDD FALDWYN
PEN DINAS
YSBYTY CYNFYN
FOUR STONES
OLD RADNOR
STRUMBLE HEAD
PENTRE IFAN
GORS FAWR
MYNYDD BACH TRECASTELL
CARREG SAMSON
CERRIG DUON
CARN GOCH
TRYLEG
ARTHUR'S STONE
CALDEY ISLAND
PARC CWM
TINKINSWOOD
NASH POINT
ST LYTHANS

In later excavations archaeologists found signs of human activity in other caves in Wales, but only in Gower has a skeleton been found. The young man of Paviland died 7,500 years before the ice started to melt, a representative to posterity of the Palaeolithic or Old Stone Age. In the difficult centuries of transition that followed the very gradual withdrawal of the ice, groups of hunters roamed the shores and hills of Wales, using small flint tools to ensure an adequate supply of food, both fish and animal. Some of these Mesolithic or Middle Stone Age microliths have been found, especially in the south-west of Wales. Some time after 6,000 BC the level of the sea, which had become swollen as the ice melted, had risen sufficiently for the land bridge with the continent to be broken, thus separating Britain from the mainland of Europe.

Neolithic Wales

> The Stone Age, the Bronze Age, the early Iron Age pass through the Welsh memory like a blurred dream ... all over Wales they have their monuments; crumbled stone villages and turf-covered forts ... burial chambers, cromlechs, and most haunting of all, the single enigmatic boulders which stand here and there all alone in empty landscapes, as markers, as memorials or perhaps as warnings.
>
> Jan Morris, *The Matter of Wales*

The forebears of those who brought the ideas that were to constitute the Neolithic revolution in Wales hailed from the three great river valleys of the Middle East, the Nile, the Tigris and the Euphrates.

Remarkable changes that occurred in those parts between 6,000 and 5,000 BC gave rise to a revolution in the pattern of living that probably had no equal in significance in the story of mankind until the Industrial Revolution changed the way of life in Europe some 250 years ago. Reduced to its basic terms, this revolution in the Middle East amounted to the development of new farming methods that were to prove so successful that for the first time in human history man was able to produce a surplus of food. This simple transforming economic fact had profound social consequences; to start with, it led to a rapid increase in population, and at the same time enabled some people to be freed from the hitherto general chore of growing food, making it possible for some to specialise in making the sort of tools for which the new farming methods cried out. These craftsmen, in order to provide these tools, needed raw materials. To supply these there came into existence a trading class, which was also drawn from the ranks of those whose services were no longer required for the production of food.

This new society that emerged from this first division of labour comprised farmers, craftsmen and traders. The fresh ideas which animated this new society passed, albeit slowly, from the Middle East to Europe, partly because the increased population looked for somewhere to live, partly because the traders were searching in distant places for supplies of the vital raw materials and partly because some farmers, having exhausted their lands, were ever on the lookout for untilled lands to bring into cultivation. The further west these Neolithic men emigrated in their varying quests, the simpler were the changes they brought, until when they finally crossed into these islands, they brought with them only the basic knowledge of mixed farming and simple skills in weaving and in making pots. In their flimsy cross-channel boats, however, were very precious cargoes indeed: sheep, cattle and the seeds of wheat. These early Neolithic men and women, who probably came in quite small groups, were the first settlers in Wales; those that were in Wales before them, the Mesolithic hunters and fishers had been nomadic in habit. They hunted and fished for a season before

1. *Goat's Hole cave, Paviland (photo: Chris Elphick)*; 2. *Mesolithic blades from Gwynedd*; 3. *Penmaenmawr axe*

Goat's Hole

moving on to stalk other quarries and search unknown streams. The Neolithic settlers, by way of contrast, lived in communities, where the general practice seems to have been for the men to look after the animals while the women were held responsible for the growing of the crops. Most of what is now known about the social life of New Stone Age people comes from the excavation of their burial places. Nomads had no cemeteries, individuals being buried where they died. The long barrow, which is the main clue today to a Neolithic settlement, is really a roofed cemetery, in fact the village burial ground.

As the infiltration into Wales of Neolithic groups probably continued for more than 2,000 years, which is twice as long a period of time as that which covers all English history since the Battle of Hastings, it is hardly surprising that there was considerable variation in the types of graves used, and indeed even in the shape of the covering mounds, which tended in the later years of Neolithic settlement to be round rather than long. Most Neolithic chambered tombs consisted of a number of burial compartments, linked by passages or galleries and roofed over with huge capstones. When such a cemetery was full it was covered over with a large mound of earth. As these early people deemed it wise to bury with their dead a selection of tools and utensils used in life, skilled modern excavation has revealed much valuable information about the Neolithic way of life.

At this stage it is necessary to introduce the topic of the druids about whom more nonsense has been written than about flying saucers! Readers who are uncertain about them are advised to read Stuart Piggot's book *The Druids*, which once and for all puts fact and fiction into proper perspective. The historical druids, who flourished in the early Iron Age, constituted a Celtic priesthood whose activities are recorded from the second century BC. Nevertheless, many a prehistoric ruin has in the public mind become associated with the druids, none more so than stone circles and bare cromlechs standing up alone on bleak moors. A cromlech, that is to say upright stones linked by a heavy capstone, is often

1. *'Druid Circle' above Penmaenmawr;*
2. *Bryn Cader Faner, Meirionnydd;*
3. *Gors Fawr stone circle, Pembrokeshire*

all that remains of a Neolithic burial place from which the covering mound has been eroded by the combined efforts of time and vandals, one surviving burial chamber bearing witness to the former cemetery that antedated the druids by several thousand years.

The earliest such communal burial places in Wales are to be found not far from the west coast, suggesting a close connection with the people who at about the same time were settling in Ireland. Pembrokeshire, Conwy and Anglesey provide excellent examples of such early burials, details of which will be given later. Suffice it here to mention four outstanding specimens, which, thanks to skilful excavation and, in two of the cases, partial restoration, can be seen and appreciated by those who possess the twin advantages of imagination and a car! Of these chosen representatives of the earliest Neolithic settlements in Wales, one is to be found in Pembrokeshire, at Pentre Ifan, on the foothills of the Preseli hills, another above the Conwy valley, at Capel Garmon, while the other two are in Anglesey: one is Bryn Celli Ddu in the south of the island, the other is Barclodiad y Gawres, near Rhosneigr, in the north-west.

Later Neolithic infiltrations into the western part of Britain, dating from about 2,000 BC, were of people from the south of Brittany, who either settled in the Cotswolds or crossed the Severn before making their homes in southern Wales. Their graves are categorised as belonging to the Severn-Cotswold type, good Welsh examples of which can be seen at Tinkinswood, which is between Cardiff and Barry (*Y Barri*), and on the Gower peninsula at Parc Cwm. At about this same time something very remarkable indeed was taking place further west into Wales in the Preseli hills, where a band of very strong Neolithic men dug out of the mountainside the so-called bluestones. These stones, which were to be found nowhere else in the British Isles, were used to form the smaller circle at Stonehenge, though how and why they were transported from the mountains of south Wales to the centre of Salisbury Plain no man yet knows.

As to Neolithic artefacts, there is considerable archaeological evidence of

1. *Bryn Celli Ddu;*
2. *Pentre Ifan; 3. Bach-wen chamber*

domestic pottery, while by the end of Neolithic times men had learned how to make drinking vessels also by using clay. The most numerous artefacts to survive are finely-made flint arrow-heads and polished stone axes. Certainly, by the middle of the New Stone Age a properly-organised trade in stone axes had been developed in northern Wales, the necessary raw materials being provided by – doubtless among others – stone axe factories in Llŷn at Mynydd Rhiw (234 299) and on the eastern end of Penmaenmawr Mountain at Graiglwyd (715 755).

The Beaker Folk

Somewhere about the beginning of the second millennium BC new immigrants came upon the scene. Those forebears had begun a long, restless trek to the west and south of the continent from the forest clearings of eastern Europe, where they had first made their appearance in about 10,000 BC. The advance parties of these strangers crossed from the mainland of Europe in about 2,000 BC and landed along the eastern and southern coasts of Britain, gradually thereafter penetrating inland. Of the very many immigrants who eventually infiltrated into Wales, large numbers may well have travelled, albeit by easy stages, via the high lands of Shropshire.

Something of the initial impact made by the arrival of these newcomers on the Neolithic inhabitants of northern Wales can be imagined from the contrast presented by their different appearance; for these people were light of hair and fair of complexion, and were much taller and much heavier than the small dark residents of northern Wales whom they were gradually to dispossess. These new settlers have sometimes been identified with the so-called Beaker Folk, whose name was derived from the distinctive cups that were foremost among their grave goods. In fact these beakers would more accurately be associated with late Neolithic men and women, but as there is unlikely to have been any clear-cut division between late Neolithic and early Bronze Age times, little damage will be done if the term Beaker Folk is applied both to late Neolithic and early Bronze Age men and women.

The association of these beakers with

1. Archaeological finds on Mynydd Rhiw;
2. Waste from an axe factory

the Bronze Age, however, cries out for an explanation, especially as most of the new arrivals brought with them no metal goods of any description, nor had they in all probability any knowledge of their existence. Nevertheless, by coming to these islands when they did, they were very soon made aware of the existence of metal objects. At that time Ireland had achieved a considerable reputation for the excellence of its metal workers, who had learned how to take full advantage of the copper deposits of Kerry and of the alluvial gold to be found in the Wicklow mountains. Knowledge of the products of these Irish smiths travelled quickly along well-known trade routes, reaching the ears of the fair-haired newcomers to Wales, who were aggressive by nature and thereafter quickly able to recognise the superiority of metal weapons over those made of stone. At this stage in their development they were more interested in the ways of war than in the paths of agricultural peace, quietly trodden by the Neolithic people. Thus Wales became an expanding export market for Irish tools and weapons, chief among which were axes and daggers of bronze; and in later Bronze Age times, when life had become rather more civilised, for Irish copper and gold ornaments and decorations.

Of the settling-in process of these people little is known beyond the bare fact that there was an initial clash in which the greater strength of the invaders gave them the mastery. There was, however, probably more infiltration than confrontation, especially as a beneficent change in climate around 2,000 BC, which resulted in warmer, drier conditions, opened up for settlement higher areas in Wales than had been available for their Neolithic predecessors. Illustrations of this are plentifully at hand in central Wales, where in the Brecon Beacons Bronze Age round barrows have been found more than 2,000 feet (610 m) above sea level. Nevertheless there is archaeological evidence, too, to prove that Bronze Age men took over existing Neolithic settlements: high up above Dyffryn Conwy the long barrow at Capel Garmon, which for so long had been the communal burial ground of a Neolithic community, revealed to twentieth-century man red fragments of a beaker that has been carbon-dated 1,500 BC. Clearly a Neolithic site had been taken over by men of the Bronze Age, just as in much later times it was again to be occupied by Iron Age settlers, who were thus to maintain a continuity of occupation at Capel Garmon.

The Bronze Age was to last in Wales for about 1,500 years; this vast expanse of time witnessed many invasions and infiltrations of new groups, coming in by a variety of routes. Settlement in Wales in the early years would probably have been sparse, but western coastal routes placed Wales on the main trade and settling roads from southern Europe. However, by about 1,500 BC, when Bronze Age culture was at its peak, a fairly clear picture emerges of Bronze Age settlements in Wales, by which time many groups had crossed the Denbighshire moors, some settling above the Dyffryn Conwy or west of the Rhinogydd mountains, while others penetrated into Llŷn or crossed into Anglesey. Other groups had ventured into central areas, settling either in the river valleys of Powys or on the hills and moorlands above, where they were to pursue their pastoralist ways – for by 1,500 BC the former warriors had become rearers of cattle and successful farmers. They seem to have been particularly attracted by the hills and valleys of

A Bronze Age beaker found at Llithfaen

eastern Wales, where today many a skyline is broken by unexcavated round barrows, which also abound in the Teme valley, north of Knighton, and around New Radnor, where at the side of the A44 may still be seen a round barrow, fittingly sited in a farmyard, indicating continuity of occupation for 2,500 years. Further into Wales, up in the Brecon Beacons National Park, at much greater heights, there is a wealth of archaeological evidence of middle Bronze Age activity, just as there is in many parts of the south-west, from the high land around Llandeilo and Llandovery, further south to the Preseli hills and to the area north of Carmarthen, just inland from the southern coast.

The contrast between Neolithic and Bronze Age man was apparent not only in their physical appearance, but also in their burial customs, for, whereas the long barrows of Neolithic times were the burial grounds of whole communities, the round barrows of the Bronze Age people, who came after them, covered one, or at most, two bodies. This change in habit reflected not only the nomadic ways of early Bronze Age settlers but also, and more importantly, the elitist nature of their social structure. For it appears that only the head man and perhaps his wife had their graves marked by an earthen mound. It is significant that long after Bronze Age man had ceased his nomadic ways, the custom of burying the dead in separate graves continued.

In the early years of the Bronze Age inhumation was still being practised, the body usually being laid on its side in a crouched position, often in a cist of small stones. A mound of earth was then thrown over it, into the sides of which, in later years, additional burials were sometimes made. By middle Bronze Age times, about 1,500 BC, cremation had taken the place of inhumation; thereafter the ashes were usually stored in cinerary urns or in clay pots. At Bryncir, 5 miles (8 km) north of Cricieth in Llŷn, on two different sites at different times cinerary urns and sepulchral clay pots have been dug up, containing not only Bronze Age ashes but also a small bronze knife and a piece of copper.

Of the religious beliefs of the Bronze Age people very little is known for certain beyond the acceptance of the idea of life after death, which is proved by their choice of grave goods. That ritual played some part in their lives can be presumed from the varying practices in vogue at different times in connection with their burials. It is thought that unlike their Neolithic predecessors, who apparently worshipped the earth, these people believed in a sky god, perhaps the sun, and probably held their religious observances in the stone circles, which are the most striking of all Bronze Age monuments and certainly the most puzzling. Professor Thom is the chief exponent of the theory that these stone circles were virtually astronomical clocks, being laid out with such precision that skilled practitioners could, from noting accurately the position of the sun, the moon and the stars, acquire valuable foreknowledge, which was of great service to sailors and farmers. Other Bronze Age survivals that may have figured prominently in their religious rituals were the solitary standing stones that are often to be found in remote places, and cup marks that have been carved on slabs of rock or on chambered tombs or occasionally on standing stones; indeed these strange marks can be found carved on almost any surface regarded by Bronze Age man as sacred.

The first Welshmen

By 1,500 BC the Bronze Age had become consolidated, its habits and customs and rituals crystallised into a more or less unified culture. The thousand years of Bronze Age culture that followed remained a well-established way of life until Celtic invaders appeared in about 500 BC. These men were to become the first Welshmen, and it was these people who introduced the Iron Age in which we still live.

About halfway through the last millennium before the Christian era, mankind was once again on the march in Europe: successive waves of new immigrants, some of whom may well have been refugees, broke against the oft-visited shores of the British Isles. Many of these newcomers, whose homes were in the south-west of Germany or in Switzerland, were the descendants of men who had forged trading links with the people of the east Mediterranean, including the Greeks, traces of whose language were present in the language they spoke. Their culture was associated with La Tène, an area in the Lake Neuchatel district of Switzerland. Their main expansion route to the north was via Belgium and the north of France

Iron Age dwellings in the Celtic hill fort, Tre'r Ceiri, Llŷn

to the British Isles, though other infiltrations were probably also taking place by sea directly from the Iberian Peninsula to southern Wales. At about the same time too other Celts, known as the Gauls, were moving south through Alpine passes to challenge first the authority of the Etruscans in northern Italy and later that of Rome itself.

At least three groups of invaders reached Wales in the early years of this new age. These people were credited in after years with having introduced the Iron Age because they were familiar with the hard metal, and had craftsmen in their midst who knew how to make tools and weapons from it. Nevertheless, it would be misleading to say that the early harbingers of this new age depended on this new metal. In fact, for a long time, in all probability, they depended far more on bronze than on iron, sources of which had first to be discovered in these islands. But whether these people concentrated on bronze or on iron, one thing is certainly true, namely that they paid far more attention to making weapons of war than to forging tools of peace. For the Celts came as warriors, and for a long time fought their way, often among rival groups of the same tribe.

The Celts came to Wales at a time of flux: to add to the confusion stirred up by the arrival of a succession of warlike tribes bent on imposing their will, there was coincidentally another climatic change, which brought much colder weather to which considerable adjustment was required. Of the Celts who eventually gained authority in Wales and who spoke a language recognisable as the ancestor of modern Welsh, four particular tribes seem to have gained the ascendancy: the Demetae and the Silures in the south of the country, and the Deceangli and the Ordovices in the north.

Thanks to the skills developed by archaeologists in excavating Neolithic and Bronze Age sites and to the interpretative powers of prehistorians, a great deal is now known about the Neolithic and Bronze Age ways of life through the patient study of their burial mounds and the grave goods contained therein. Men of the Iron Age unfortunately paid little attention to ritual in disposing of their dead; in consequence, little had been gleaned from their burial places. In the Iron Age there were no field monuments corresponding to the barrows, the standing stones and the great stone circles of earlier cultures, though admittedly Iron Age people were very expert at fortifying their settlements, a topic that will be dealt with later. However, despite the lack of field monuments, other than hill forts, much is known about life in the Iron Age because the Iron Age was overlapped by the Roman conquest of Britain. Roman chroniclers, in the persons of the general Julius Caesar and the historian Tacitus, put much on record about the Celts, who dared to oppose their rule in the last century before the Christian era and in the first after it started, by which time the Celtic occupation of Wales was thorough and complete. Of life in Celtic Wales in the centuries before the Romans came to conquer and to chronicle, very little is known, though it is clear that they changed the pattern of agricultural settlement.

The Celtic Way of Life

The Celts for the first time imposed on the countryside of Wales a clear pattern of

Recreated Celtic **crannog** *at Llangorse lake*

settlement, a pattern which was to be dominated and controlled by what are called forts, the types of which varied considerably according to the requirements of differing geographical locations. In previous cultures the land set apart for the cultivation of food was little more than scratched because of the limitations imposed by digging sticks and hand hoes. The meagre crops produced by these primitive methods caused farmers frequently to move on, to cultivate virgin plots of land. The Celts changed all this: to start with, once they had found convenient sources of the precious new metal, iron, they could make stronger agricultural implements. Furthermore, by this time they had learned how to make a rudimentary plough, to which the Celts harnessed a pair of oxen. Thus the rectangular Celtic field system was established, whose chief social consequence was the abandoning by farmers of their previous nomadic habits.

The farmers thereafter settled near their fields, built themselves huts and gradually coalesced into communities. Their fields were usually bounded by walls made from the stones turned up in the ploughing. This new Celtic pattern of farming in the early centuries of the Iron Age thus gave rise to something approaching a social revolution. A real change in relationship developed between the people and their land, resulting in a quite different way of life. This new social format required proper protection, which was to be afforded by a vast number of forts of differing kinds in differing situations.

Of the very large number of such protected sites to be found in Wales most are quite small, enclosing probably less than one hectare (about 2½ acres), but their very number must prompt an enquiry as to the reason for the need for protection on so wide a scale. Against whom were the settlers protecting themselves? Intense tribal rivalry, in the absence of any central authority (such as before very long the Romans were to try to impose), plus the ability afforded by the possession of iron weapons to mount an attack, probably accounted for the proliferation of these forts. In hilly districts much use was made of natural defensive advantages, such as spurs and outcrops of rock, which acted as ramparts, while occasionally pointed stones were set close together by the defenders to act as an additional deterrent to any invader. Such a device is known as a *chevaux de frise*, an excellent example of which is to be seen on the Pen y Gaer fort in the Conwy valley.

In coastal areas defences were usually required only on the landward side; as an example of such a promontory fort, Nash Point in Glamorgan may be cited (915 684). While practically nothing of the interior has survived the erosion of the centuries, the entrance is still clear. Any would-be attacker would have had to overcome a succession of four ramparts before gaining access to the track which led to the actual entrance, which presumably would have been well guarded. Two of the commonest type of hill forts have been selected for special comment: one, Ffrith Faldwyn, because it was in use for a very long time, the other, Tre'r Ceiri, because it not only looks very impressive

1. & 3. Dinllugwy Celtic homestead, Anglesey; 2. Pen y Gaer

but also because it does so much to increase our knowledge of an Iron Age community.

First to Montgomery, which is worth a visit on several counts. It is a small Georgian town from which noise and bustle have ebbed. The Post Office serves also as a draper's shop and the early closing day is Saturday! Above the well-cared for little town is a castle on a hill, which still dominates the landscape as it has done for centuries. Behind and above the castle is another hill, today well-wooded, Ffrith Faldwyn, the site of many a habitation. Its origins were Neolithic, but in the third century BC the Celts arrived to add to the defences of the hill a double palisade. Archaeologists who have found four more Iron Age fortifications on the hill, attribute the last of them to the sudden threat posed by the arrival of the Romans in the neighbourhood in about 50 AD. Enough has been excavated to enable an appreciation to be made of three centuries of Iron Age activity there.

Tre'r Ceiri is to the layman the most interesting of all Iron Age forts. Yr Eifl (incorrectly anglicized to 'The Rivals') is a mountain of three peaks at the eastern end of Llŷn; the most easterly of these three peaks is Tre'r Ceiri, appropriately named, meaning the 'town of the giants'. Here at a height of more than 1,800 feet (550 m) is to be seen an astonishing survival of Celtic building in Wales. The fort is long and narrow, about 800 feet (243 m) in length and about 300 feet (92 m) wide; its walls are surprisingly well-preserved, about 6 feet (1.8 m) thick in some places, and here and there between 10 and 15 feet (4–5 m) high. Remarkable, however, as are these walls and the three postern gates in them, pride of place must be given to the 150 huts in the space enclosed by the walls; their varying shapes from circular to square help to confirm the theory that their building was spread over several centuries. Dating the fort is difficult but it seems certain that it remained inhabited throughout the Roman occupation of Britain.

The Druids

The Romans, whose initial reconnaisance on the shores of southern Britain in 55 BC was followed by an army of occupation in 43 AD, entered Wales in about 50 AD Their conquest was opposed by the Celts, who were sufficiently well-organised to constitute a threat to Roman plans. The

Silures in the south and the Ordovices in the north, by their spirited resistance, reminded the Romans of the trouble they had previously experienced at the hands of the Celts in their earlier conquest of Gaul. The further the Celts were from the centre of Roman government, the greater was their determination to resist. Hence it was that the Roman general Suetonius Paulinus set himself the task of subduing Anglesey, the very centre of Celtic resistance and the headquarters of druidism.

The druids were a priestly caste of Celts whose leadership, though basically spiritual, had spread over into the realm of political power. According to Tacitus, potential Celtic leaders were sent from distant Celtic domains in Europe to Anglesey, where they were taught and trained and indoctrinated in druid lore, which had become the official religion of all Celts everywhere. These druid leaders seemingly constituted a hierarchy of enormous importance; they taught religion and astronomy, history and philosophy and were held in the greatest veneration by the rest of the Celts, over whom they exercised a very tight discipline. Unfortunately for posterity, however, all their teaching was oral, which left the way clear for romantics down the centuries to indulge their imaginations. In fact, practically nothing is known of what the druids taught. All that is known for certain is that the Celts in Wales, thanks to their druid advisers in Anglesey, were utterly opposed to the overlordship of Rome, and that the Romans decided in consequence to destroy druidism root and branch.

In 61 AD Suetonius Paulinus, with more than a little trepidation, crossed into Anglesey and advanced upon the sacred groves of the druids in the middle of the island, where he burned all the trees and killed all the priests. He was recalled from this act of butchery by news of Boudicca's rising in eastern Britain. Although he had not succeeded in breaking the power of the Celts, he had destroyed their power base, the priesthood of the druids.

The Archaeological Record

The most ancient surviving sites in Wales of human habitations, however temporary, are to be found in north-eastern Wales. Earliest of all, carbon-dated to about 180,000 BC is near Y Bontnewydd, is a cave, about 4 miles (6.5 km) north-west of Denbigh and 3 miles (4.8 km) south-west of St Asaph, the grid reference being 015 710. This cave, which is not normally open to the public, is cut into the limestone cliff which dominates the north side of the Elwy. First excavated in 1872, it has in recent years been thoroughly surveyed by the National Museum of Wales. Many implements, mostly made of quartzite, have been found there together with some human bones.

A few miles further east lies the village of Tremeirchion, a mile south of which are to be found two important caves, very near to each other. One is called Ffynnon Beuno, the other Cae Gwyn (085 724). Both sites, when excavated about a hundred years ago, yielded up a few human and a great many animal bones; the caves are thought to have been the homes of hyenas, many of whose bones have survived along with the remains of the animals they killed, like woolly rhinoceros and mammoth. In addition flint implements were also found which enabled archaeologists to give a date to the site somewhere between 50,000 and 30,000 BC. Cae Gwyn is now quite

inaccessible but with care Ffynnon Beuno may be explored.

Palaeolithic remains in Gower are of much more recent habitations than those of the limestone caves of the north. 16,500 BC is the approximate date given to the earliest human being found on the Gower peninsula, that of the skeleton of the young Cro-Magnon man, formerly known as the Red Lady of Paviland; the grid reference for the Goat's Hole, where it was found, is 437 858. Paviland lies east of Worms Head in the south of the peninsula along the coast between Rhosili and Port Einion. Access to this cave is from the shore, but only at low tide. It appears to have been used by man and beast for a great many years, the earliest animal occupation probably antedating the arrival of humans there by about 10,000 years, while archaeological evidence also suggests much later occupation in Mesolithic, Neolithic and even in Roman times.

Also on the Gower peninsula a visit is recommended to Cat Hole (538 900), an

1. Llugwy burial chamber, Anglesey;
2. Exterior of Y Bontnewydd cave; 3. Maen
y Bardd cromlech above the Conwy valley

inland rock shelter above a wooded valley, north-west of Oxwich in the parish of Ilston. The earliest occupation is thought to have been about 10,000 BC. It appears from the evidence afforded by numerous flints found there that a substantial flint industry flourished there in late Palaeolithic times. There have been a number of excavations of the site from which it has been deduced that Mesolithic men also sheltered there in later years, while later again men of the Bronze Age chose to bury their dead in this rock shelter.

As the ice melted (somewhere around 9,000 BC), the weather gradually became warmer, and the vegetation grew lush and in consequence the caves and rock shelters became dark and wet and no longer habitable. Men and women had to leave their homes and somehow learn how to adjust to the changed environment. These so-called Mesolithic or Middle Stone Age people were hunters who came to depend for their survival on killing the new animals that had been attracted by the deciduous woodland that had spread as the ice retreated. Of these animals the most important were the red deer. Man had by this time acquired sufficient technique to make small sharp barbs from their flakes of flint. Armed with these microliths, which they attached to sticks, they hunted down the deer that roamed the woodland. Small collections of these microliths have been found both in north-eastern Wales and in Glamorgan. Those found at Rhuddlan in Denbighshire have been carbon-dated to about 6,500 BC while those discovered near Prestatyn are thought to have been fashioned about 1,500 years later.

High up under the Denbigh Moors the deliberate flooding of the Brenig valley was completed in 1976 (985 576). Fortunately, the architects of the scheme took archaeologists into their confidence; the result was that very valuable prehistoric sites were not only identified and excavated but also protected for posterity. A sunny day spent at Llyn Brenig reservoir will reveal to the discerning visitor many prehistoric sites of widely differing periods and cultures. A series of trails have been devised with accompanying maps and markers. From the central car park one of these trails leads to a Mesolithic summer camp, suitably marked.

In a later section the short sea crossing

from Tenby in Pembrokeshire to Caldey Island will be strongly recommended in order to study some early Christian memorial stones of outstanding interest. This same holy island (it is now the home of a monastic community, members of which are well-disposed towards historically-minded visitors) also possesses a number of Mesolithic sites, amongst which are Nanna's Cave (145 960) and Porter's Cave (143 971).

Very many Neolithic sites have been identified in Wales, some of which now only exist in vestigial traces. In this section a selection has been made, in compiling which attention has been given both to their intrinsic interest and to their geographical spread. Moving from north to south, the first sites to be mentioned are those in Anglesey, where there are so many that it is invidious to make a choice.

Halfway up the east coast of the island, behind Benllech, lies the village of Ty'n-y-gongl, above which on rising ground is Pant-y-saer (509 824). It has been excavated twice; there remains today a large sloping capstone, supported by low stones, which cover a burial pit cut into the rock. Here more than 40 skeletons were found, and some Neolithic pottery.

On the opposite coast, a mile and a half south-east of Holyhead, between the A5 and B4545, is the long barrow Trefignath (258 805). A car may be left about 100 yards (91 m) from the site, which until recently was regarded as a good example of a passage grave, subdivided into several chambers, the whole being similar to segmented graves found in parts of Ireland and in the south of Scotland. This view was supported by the visual remains which principally consist of two 7-feet-high (2 m) portal stones and a passage some 45 feet (13.7 m) long leading from it. There is little sign of a covering mound that was noted by observers a hundred years ago. Another excavation between 1977 and 1979 suggested, however, that the grave is not all of one piece. While it is still believed that the tall portal stones and at least part of the passage belong to an originally mound-covered Neolithic long barrow, other remains point to simple burials of other periods.

Of other Neolithic sites in that neighbourhood one is less than a mile (1.6 km) north of Llanfaelog, off A4080, about 2 miles (3.2 km) inland from Rhosneigr. Tŷ Newydd (344 738) consists mainly of a large capstone which rests on three

uprights. When excavated in 1935, under a fallen stone on the floor were found, amongst other things, sufficient pieces of post-Neolithic pottery to indicate that the Neolithic grave was either still in use in the Bronze Age or had been brought back into use by Bronze Age men.

Not far south of Rhosneigr and 2 miles (3.2 km) north-west of Aberffraw is one of the most important and visually striking Neolithic sites in the whole of Britain, Barclodiad y Gawres (328 708), which is not to be confused with another burial site with an identical name in Gwynedd on the Roman road between Caerhun and Segontium (716 716). Anglesey's Barclodiad y Gawres has had to be locked up. The burial chamber can now be visited by appointment every Saturday, Sunday and Bank Holiday Monday between 12 and 4 pm from 1 April until 31 October. Visitors should call into the nearby Wayside Stores in Llanfaelog, one mile (1.6 km) north of the chamber, and they will be accompanied to the chamber by a member of staff. The burial chamber can be viewed externally throughout the year between 10am and 4pm (apart from 24-26 December and 1 January).

Barclodiad y Gawres is wonderfully situated on a headland overlooking Cable Bay where a car may be left on the foreshore below, before following the signpost which points to the headland a quarter of a mile (0.4 km) away. The burial chamber, which was thoroughly excavated in 1953, has been skilfully restored, and in the process a concrete dome has been built over it to protect its precious contents from the weather and the wickedness of man. It is essential to take a torch. The grave itself is of the normal Neolithic passage type, giving access to a central area on one side of which is a single small chamber and on the other a double one. Unfortunately many stones had been stolen and a great deal of damage done in the years before the excavation took place. What makes the place so exciting today is the survival there of five upright stones with chevrons, spirals and zigzags carved on their surfaces. The stone carvers will have had a cultural affinity with those who settled in Spain and Ireland. The stones themselves are thought to have been glacial erratics, deposited on the headland.

The last Neolithic site on Anglesey

1. Barclodiad y Gawres; 2. Arthur's Stone, Gower; 3. Dyffryn Ardudwy earmarked for special comment is probably the best known and most famous, Bryn Celli Ddu (508 702). It is perhaps best to approach it via the A5, turning left at Llanfair Pwllgwyngyll on to the A4080. A mile (1.6 km) along this road turn right on to a minor road, marked Llanddaniel-fab. Before this village is reached a marker will be seen on the right-hand side indicating a field track which is barred to cars, leading to Bryn Celli Ddu. The site is open daily from 10 am to 4 pm (apart from 24, 25 and 26 December and 1 January), last admission half an hour before closing.

Once inside the fenced-in enclosure a restored circular mound is visible. Access through the locked iron door is to a passage grave, in the central chamber of which stands a smooth-faced stone pillar. On the outside of the mound at the back may be seen in a shallow pit a stone (a replica of the original which is housed in the National Museum of Wales in Cardiff). This stone has spirals and other decorative patterns carved on it, reminiscent of Barclodiad y Gawres. The pit, which is likely to have witnessed important rituals, originally marked the very middle of the monument.

The visitor who wants to acquire some sense of the size and significance of this outstanding prehistoric monument should climb on to the top of the mound and realise that the original mound would have covered the whole of the area now enclosed by the wire fence. Bryn Celli Ddu may well have been, as well as a cemetery, an important meeting place. Neolithic men first came here to bury their dead, but equally certainly, Bronze Age people continued to use the same site for very many years, so that it should be regarded today as much a monument of the Bronze Age as of the New Stone Age.

Between Anglesey and the south, which were the two great centres of early prehistoric settlement in Wales, three Neolithic sites claim special attention, of which the most northerly is Capel Garmon (818 542). This burial place occupies a remote site, high up on the eastern side of the Conwy valley, well above the road which runs from Betws-y-coed to Llanrwst. Half a mile (0.8 km) of country road south-west of the village of Capel Garmon leads to a widened stretch where a car may be left. A fingerpost points to a farm where the necessary pamphlet may be obtained, and to the site, which enjoys a spectacular view of the distant hills the other side of the valley.

This Neolithic long barrow is shaped like a wedge, a horned forecourt at the east end luring unwanted strangers in former times to a false entrance, the true approach is from the south via a passage, at the end of which were two burial chambers, one to the west, the other to the east. The excavation of 1924 revealed, along with Neolithic remains, sufficient pottery to prove that Bronze Age people continued to use the site long after Neolithic men and women had passed from the scene.

Capel Garmon long barrow

The next site to be explored is near the A496, the coast road which goes from Harlech to Barmouth. Just south of the village of Dyffryn Ardudwy the remains of the long barrow, bearing the same name, can be found behind the village school (589 229). This is indeed a place of stones, suggesting that the burial place here was roofed with stones rather than by the usual grassy mounds of earth. There are remains of two burial places. The smaller, earlier one is the more westerly, its outline clearly marked out in the stones on the ground. The other, slightly later, was much bigger. It is probable that one roof of stones would have covered both graves, in which archaeologists have found early Neolithic pottery.

In western Powys, in central Wales, is an unusual long barrow, unusual because it is perched up on the edge of a ridge, Tŷ Illtud (reference to this name will be made later when the Celtic church is under consideration). The actual site (098 263) is in a field belonging to Manest Farm, which is situated a mile (1.6 km) up a minor road which leaves the A40 4 miles (6.5 km) south-east of Brecon at the village of Scethrog. Permission must be sought at the farm to visit the site, which is visible from the lane, a brisk walk away up the hill. Special interest is centred on the partly-roofed forecourt and the wallstones on which have been carved, probably in medieval times, patterns which in the course of time have greatly exercised the minds and imaginations of many visitors.

Moving south into Pembrokeshire, pride of place must go to Pentre Ifan (099 370) 7 miles (11.25 km) south-west of Cardigan; it stands in a field, near a lane, roughly equidistant between the A487 and the B4329. The surviving entrance to this

Carreg Samson, Pembrokeshire

chambered tomb consists of three pillars, 8 feet (2.43 m) high, surmounted by an immense capstone, 16 feet (4.87 m) long, in front of which is a forecourt, semicircular in shape. The covering mound will have been about 130 feet (40 m) long. The unusual orientation was north-south, as it also was at Tŷ Illtud. Traces of ritual pits are visible, the purpose of which is frequently guessed at, but at this distance of time hardly likely to be known.

Neolithic remains abound in the coastal area between Strumble Head and St David's, suggesting a safe anchorage and considerable settlement. Let one such site speak for them all, Carreg Samson (846 334) in the parish of Mathry, lying 7 miles (11.25 km) to the south-west of Fishguard, near Abercastle, and occupying a splendid position overlooking the bay. Today all that remains of a long barrow, which originally was probably covered by stones rather than by grass, are seven upright stones, roofed by a capstone. Inland along this coast another ten similar Neolithic sites may be found.

Three more Neolithic sites to be visited are further east, in Glamorgan. The first of these is on the Gower peninsula, an area which is rich in archaeological remains. Parc Cwm (537 898) is a long barrow of the Severn-Cotswold type, situated inland on the peninsula between the B4271 and A4118. First recognised as a Neolithic burial place in 1869, in 1960 it was thoroughly and scientifically excavated. On a north-south alignment, it has a forecourt shaped like a bell, which gives access to a central gallery off which are four side-chambers. Over the years the bones of about 24 people have been recovered, suggesting that Parc Cwm was a communal burial place: a cemetery with a roof on. It is a spectacular site.

The other two sites, Tinkinswood and St Lythan's, are near each other, a few miles to the west of Cardiff and south of the road which runs westwards from Cardiff to Cowbridge. Tinkinswood (092 732) was excavated in 1914 and afterwards carefully restored. The burial chamber is covered by an immense capstone, believed to be the largest in Britain, measuring 22 feet (6.7 m) by 15 feet (4.57 m); the bones of about 50 people were found, along with flints, pottery and a quantity of animal bones – the presence of the latter arguing the likelihood of funeral feasting. In the mound was discovered another of those mysterious pits, often come across in long barrows, mysterious because no one knows anything about them. Tinkinswood was probably a late Neolithic burial place, which was subsequently re-used by men of the early Bronze Age some of whose pottery has been unearthed there.

A mile to the south-east is the long barrow of St Lythan's (101 723) a visit to which may be justified by its proximity to Tinkinswood. The elements have here reduced the original long mound of stones to three uprights supporting a capstone, which stands out gauntly in the middle of a field. The site is open daily from 10 am to 4 pm (apart from 24, 25 and 26 December and 1 January), last admission half an hour before closing.

There are no surviving Bronze Age settlements in Wales: the four types of visual evidence all have to do with ritual and death, three of them posing as yet unsolved mysteries concerning the reasons why Bronze Age people periodically foregathered in stone circles, why they set up in lonely places solitary tall stones, and why they carved on some of their monuments curious shapes to which archaeologists have given the name

'cupmarks'. Their places of burial were much smaller and less complicated than those of the Neolithic people they supplanted; most of such places in Wales are simple mounds or piles of stones under which were found human bones that were buried in the early years of the Bronze Age, cremation taking over in about 1,500 BC. Sometimes the bones, cremated or otherwise, accompanied by simple grave goods such as flint knives or beads or small drinking vessels, were placed in stone cists, the walls of which consisted of large slabs. The covering

Tinkinswood burial chamber, Glamorgan

mounds of these round barrows were of grass-topped soil or of stone. Their distribution was widespread, both on hilltops and in fertile valleys, though there seems to have been something of a concentration in one part of north-western Wales. Bronze Age remains of various sorts have been unearthed at Penrhyndeudraeth, on the slopes of Cnicht, around Bryncir, at Beddgelert and at Dolwyddelan, prompting the theory that the area around the Glaslyn estuary was a major Bronze Age settlement. Today's visitor has to bear in mind that the Glaslyn was a wide tidal river that flowed as far east as the western slopes of Cnicht until the early years of the nineteenth century. Then W. A. Madocks built an embankment across the mouth of the estuary to link Meirionnydd to the Caernarfonshire side and make possible the development of a harbour at Porthmadog.

In addition to round barrows there are a number of other Bronze Age burial sites consisting of a mound or several mounds, surrounded by a ditch and bank; to such the name of 'Wessex bell-barrow' is given. The people responsible for creating these burial mounds are thought to have had strong cultural ties with a prosperous Bronze Age culture centred in Wessex. Remains of some of these bell-barrows are to be found in Glamorgan, especially in the district around Llantwit Major in the south, though there is an outstanding example in the north of the county, Crug-yr-Afan (920 954). Oddly enough there is a bell-barrow in northern Wales too, in the hilly country behind Llanfairfechan, Cors y Carneddau (723 746).

The hilly uplands of north-eastern Wales and Powys are still dotted with unexcavated round barrows, but a great many have been obliterated in the course of the centuries by the weather and the plough. In Gwynedd the energetic hill walker who climbs up westward out of the Conwy valley to walk along the ridge from Foel Grach towards the sea will be rewarded with the sight of two round barrows, one near the top of Drum, Carnedd Penyborth-goch (708 696), and another a mile or so (1.6 km) further on, Carnedd y Ddelw (708 705).

Another rewarding but less tiring excursion may be undertaken in the Denbigh Moors in Denbighshire, where a few years ago the northern part of the Brenig valley was flooded by the then

Welsh Water Authority. During the building of the reservoir archaeologists were called in who identified and excavated many Bronze Age sites, some of which have been restored and resited north-east of Llyn Brenig, where they form part of a carefully laid out trail, starting at the car park. There are other Bronze Age sites in the park, which are described and routed in a brochure obtainable at the visitor centre behind the car park.

One more round barrow, quite differently sited, is worth a mention – and a visit, though it involves a steep walk along a mountain path. The visitor to the excellent Mountain Centre at Libanus will see on the eastern horizon the twin peaks of the Brecon Beacons. The barrow, Corn Du, where a cist has been excavated, is at a height of 2,863 feet (872 m), on the side of the western summit (007 213).

Stone circles are always associated with the Bronze Age, even though nothing is known for certain about what went on within their undoubtedly sacred confines. Wales has nothing to offer to compare with the magnificence of Castlerigg near Keswick or of Long Meg near Penrith, but there are a number of small stone circles still surviving, most concentrated in the hilly uplands of Powys. Jaquetta Hawkes says this of them:

> looking at them in the loneliness and grandeur of the mountain country in which they so often stand we have to imagine them a centre of movement, colour, vitality and emotion.

Three such circles in the mountain country west and south-west of Brecon may be visited in one day, of which the most southerly and the best is Cerrig Duon (852 206), which stands out at a height of 1,270 feet (387 m), not far from the source of the river Tawe. The circle consists of 22 stones (there are about eight gaps); none of the stones is higher than about 18 inches (0.45 m), the whole perimeter measuring about 190 feet (58 m). About 30 feet (9 m) north of the circle is a large standing stone about 6 feet (1.8 m) high, while north-east of the circle are two nearly parallel rows of stones. This alignment clearly stood in some relationship to the circle.

Six miles (9.65 km) north of Cerrig Duon and a quarter of a mile (0.4 km) to the east of the Roman camp at Y Pigwn is Mynydd Bach Trecastell (833 310). It is usually permissible to visit the site, although it is actually inside the boundary of the army training centre. Here two circles will be found, the smaller one to the south being 24 feet (7.31 m) in diameter, the larger 76 feet (23 m). There is, as at Cerrig Duon, an alignment of stones, leading away from the southern circle in a south-westerly direction.

The third site lies 3 miles (4.8 km) further south and 1.5 miles (2.4 km) south of the Usk Reservoir, Nant Tarw (819 258), which has to be approached on foot over rather rough moorland. Again there are two enclosures, of which one is circular with seven uprights still in position, while the other, elliptical in shape, has 12 surviving stones of which the tallest is 3.5 feet (1 m) high.

North-western Anglesey provides a number of standing stones that are typical enough to speak for the rest that can be seen in many different parts of Wales. At Pen yr Orsedd (333 903 and 333 906) are two specimens, 6 to 7 feet (1.8–2.1 m) high, while 1¾ miles (2.8 km) north-north-east of Bodedern is another at Tregwehelydd. The stone here, which is 8.5 feet (2.6 m) high, was found in three pieces but is now bolted together. On the nearby Holy Island will be found two more sites, one Tŷ Mawr (254 810), a mile (1.6 km) south-south-east of Holyhead has a 9 foot (2.75 m) stone, while at Penrhosfeilw (227809), 1¾ miles (2.8 km) south-west of Holyhead there are two stones, 11 feet (3.35 m) apart, each about 10 feet (3 m) high.

Near Devil's Bridge in the most northerly part of Ceredigion is the little nineteenth-century church of Ysbyty Cynfyn, which seems to have been built in the middle of a Bronze Age site. Today's churchyard wall contains five stones, which were part of the original Bronze Age alignment; two of them have been moved to act as gate-posts, while the other three, one of which is about 10 feet (3 m) high, have probably remained undisturbed since they were first erected 3,500 years ago.

Far away in Powys, near the old boundary between Radnorshire and Herefordshire, a few hundred yards north of the A44 at 245 608, are the Four Stones. These are glacial boulders, set up with their flat surfaces facing the middle. No one knows why they were put up nor what happened there, but half a mile (0.8 km) away to the north-east is another similar group of glacial erratics (262 609).

While in the neighbourhood a further

visit is recommended, namely to Old Radnor, which lies one mile (1.6 km) to the south of the Four Stones. Old Radnor today consists only of a church, an inn and a few houses, but a visit is well worth while to view one of the biggest and certainly the best parish church in Radnorshire, to ponder on the possible prehistoric origin of what today is the font of the church and above all to marvel at the fact that the church stands on top of Bronze Age earthworks.

Of the mysteries which surround Bronze Age practices none is harder to comprehend than the reason for the so-called cupmarks which were carved on a variety of stone surfaces, though it seems possible that they played some part in burial ritual. Three sites are suggested for visits, one in Llŷn, another near the Pembrokeshire coast, and the third in Gwent in the village of Tryleg below Monmouth.

Near Clynnog Fawr, the St David's of northern Wales, is a long barrow; on the upper surface of its capstone are no fewer than 110 cupmarks. Bach-wen (407 495) is far from easy to find. It is sited on private land with no fingerpost to offer guidance.

The lane to the west of the church runs to the coast; two-thirds of the way along it is a 'cross-lane'. Take the lane to the left which finishes at a gate, beyond which the cromlech may be seen. The search is worth the effort because Bach-wen presents an interesting situation. The mound, be it of soil or stone, that originally covered this Neolithic burial place, must have disappeared by Bronze Age times for Bronze Age men to be able to carve their cupmarks on top of the capstone. A similar situation may be observed at Trelyffant (082 425) in Pembrokeshire. West of the B4582, which runs south-west from Cardigan to Nevern, lie the remains of a long barrow whose capstone reveals 22 cupmarks.

Finally, to the west side of the Wye valley in Gwent, where Tryleg is situated. This was at one time the county town of Monmouthshire (Mynwy) and in more recent times famed as the birthplace of Bertrand Russell. Tryleg takes its name

1. Penrhosfeilw stones, Anglesey; 2. Largest Bronze Age cairn in Wales on the summit of Carnguwch, Llŷn; 3. Trefigneth burial chamber, Anglesey

from the three stones which have been anachronistically linked with the Saxon Harold, who made war in these parts. Harold's Stones (499 051) belong to the Bronze Age and lean in different directions, with the middle one bearing two cupmarks on its southern side.

Penmaenmawr and Great Orme

Surprisingly, researches to prehistoric sites in Wales have revealed that there were thriving industries here from an early age.

The granite rock of Penmaenmawr on the northern coast was ideal for making hafted stone axes over 5,000 years ago. The rock was quarried at Graiglwyd (715 755) above the present village and would be flaked and polished into a suitable blade, and then bound to a wooden handle. These axes were prized possessions, being symbols of authority and identity which were passed down through the generations. They are proof of the growth of a prehistoric industry and examples have been found hundreds of miles from Penmaenmawr.

Beneath the limestone headland of Great Orme (772 831), at the northern end of Llandudno bay, people discovered the remarkable properties of copper nearly 4,000 years ago. This copper ore, when combined with tin could be smelted and forged into bronze tools and weapons – a huge breakthrough in human technology. Extraction of the ore was difficult and would have required considerable expertise. Vast caverns were dug by miners using nothing more than stone and bone tools. These prehistoric mines are of global historical significance – most of the tunnels have only been uncovered since the late-1980s. But in that time they have revealed an enormous amount about how our prehistoric ancestors drew on these rich veins of ore below ground and changed the world above forever. Today, there is an extended Visitor Centre at the Great Orme Mines, offering the remarkable experience of underground tours to the lives and work of the prehistoric miners.

Enough has been said about Ffridd Faldwyn and Tre'r Ceiri, the two outstanding Iron Age settlements in Wales, to limit reference here to only their geographical positions. Ffridd Faldwyn (216 969) is half a mile (0.8 km) west of Montgomery, while Tre'r Ceiri (374 447) looms up above the A449, which links

Caernarfon to Pwllheli, just after the road leaves the north coast, south-west of Clynnog Fawr.

For holidaymakers in Anglesey a visit to Dinllugwy is a very rewarding experience. Cars may be left at Llanallgo, north of Benllech, from where a walk of little more than half a mile (0.8 km) in a northerly direction will reveal first a Neolithic long barrow, then the interesting ruins of a twelfth-century church (with a crypt under the chancel), and finally after a pleasant approach through a wood, a well-hidden Celtic village. Dinllugwy (496 862) is not the usual type of Iron Age fortification, but rather a native village which seems to have been fortified at a later stage in its existence, probably in the fourth century AD. The half-acre site was enclosed by walls, 4–5 feet (1.2–1.5 m) thick, which formed a pentagon. There are the remains of two circular houses and a number of rectangular enclosures, thought to have been used for the smelting of iron.

Another Iron Age fort lies about 3 miles (4.8 km) inland from Y Felinheli on the north Wales coast, north-east of Caernarfon. The actual site of Dinas Dinorwig (550 653) is in the uplands a mile (1.6 km) south of Llanddeiniolen (on B4366). This Iron Age settlement is likely to have been in use for several centuries, the first settlers having probably dug themselves in before the Romans reached Wales. The subsequent enlarging and strengthening of the fort may well have been occasioned by the building of the Roman station at Segontium, 5 miles (8 km) to the south-west, which Dinas Dinorwig overlooked. Although the place is now very much overgrown, there is enough left to suggest that this was a substantial hill fort.

The next hill fort, Craig Rhiweirth (057 270) beckons only to the adventurous. It is situated on a hilltop, overlooking the Tanat valley in mid-Wales, about a mile (1.6 km) north of Llangynog, which lies on the B4391, a useful place for leaving a car. On the way up to the top disused lead mines will be seen, which in the eighteenth century produced much high quality ore. The summit, where Iron Age Celts chose to settle, is more than adequately protected by nature on all but the north side. Within the defences, both man-made and natural, are to be seen the remains of a large number of stone huts, mostly facing south, in all probability amounting to about 150, but the site has not yet been thoroughly excavated.

Just south of Aberystwyth is a hill on whose upper slopes the first settlers in these parts made their homes. Pendinas (584 805) has two peaks, which these Celts fortified separately in about 300 BC, adding in later years a wall which was to enclose them both. The site was apparently occupied for about 200 years. Today these Iron Age remains share the somewhat incongruous company of a column, consisting of an upended cannon, put there to commemorate victory at Waterloo.

The last site to be dealt with in this section overlooks the Tywi valley, in Carmarthenshire. Carn Goch (691 243), situated about 5 miles (8 km) north east of Llandeilo and about 3 miles (4.8 km) south of Llangadog, is one of the largest hill forts in south Wales. It is over 2,000 feet (610 m) long and about 500 feet (152 m) wide; part of the defensive wall stands in places over 20 feet (6 m) high. Despite its ruinous state this fort still impresses, especially as four gateways are still visible, all lined with upright slabs of stone.

Great Orme's Bronze Age Copper Mine

Roman Interlude

Roman penetration and organisation

The raid into Anglesey made by Suetonius Paulinus in 61 AD has to be seen as an isolated punitive raid, forced upon the Romans by their very real fear of the influence exercised by the druid priesthood over the Celts, who were putting up such stout resistance to Roman arms in other parts of southern Britain. The systematic conquest and occupation of Wales could not be attempted until the rest of southern Britain had first been made to toe the line. Hence, although the Roman invaders had landed in Kent in 43 AD, it was not until 74 AD that the systematic conquest of Wales could be contemplated. In that year Sextus Julius Frontinus succeeded to the governorship of Britain, and wasted little time before mounting an attack against the Silures, whose territory roughly corresponded to Gwent and Glamorgan. Two miles (3.2 km) north-east of modern Newport, Frontinus made a base and established a military fortress, *Isca Silurum* (Caerleon), where he quartered the second Augustan legion, 5,600 strong. From Isca he attacked the Silures, who proved to be doughty fighters as the Roman historian Tacitus confirmed. 'He [Frontinus] defeated the Silures, a strong and aggressive tribe, overcoming a brave enemy and a difficult terrain.' In the course of this campaign Frontinus seems to have established bases on tidal estuaries at Neath and Loughor, from which vantage points he was able to provision and reinforce the soldiers in the field. The lands further west than those occupied by the Silures were controlled by the Demetae, whose tribal capital was Carmarthen. The absence of any considerable ruin of Roman fortifications in modern Pembrokeshire and Carmarthenshire suggests that the Demetae presented a lesser military threat to the invaders. The plans and tactics so successfully used by Frontinus in the conquest of Silurian south Wales, however, became models for subsequent imitation when the reduction of the more northerly Ordovices was under consideration.

Four years later Gnaeus Julius Agricola took over from Frontinus and immediately

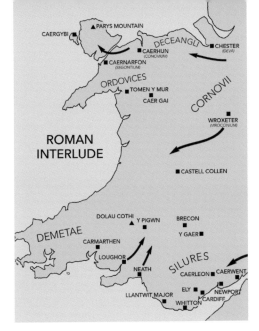

roads and choosing suitable sites for fortifying. One of these forts was established the following year, 75 AD, 4½ miles (7.24 km) up the Conwy valley at Caerhun, which was in later days to be linked with other strong points further south like Tomen y Mur. Caerhun's main importance, however, was as a staging post on the road to a bigger fort to be built further west, which Agricola selected and had built in the year 78 AD on high ground above Caernarfon. This remote fort was *Segontium*, from where the campaign to conquer Anglesey was in the same year launched and speedily brought to a successful conclusion.

Important sites

It is of course one thing for an invading force to conquer a territory; quite another to administer it adequately. The Romans, however, were nothing if not thorough and painstaking, and they had had a great deal of experience with occupation policy elsewhere. The Romans, throughout their long occupation of Wales supervised and controlled the conquered lands from two legionary fortresses, from Chester in the north – which kept under its watchful

set about the subjugation of the Ordovices. The Deceangli, who inhabited north-eastern Wales, having already been subdued, one assumes, fairly easily, insofar as there are no traces of Roman forts thereabouts. In 74 AD Agricola sent out parties of soldiers from Chester, which was the headquarters of the twentieth legion. Each party consisted of from 500 to 1,000 men, who methodically marched westwards, pausing to build the necessary

glance the Deceangli and the Ordovices – and from Caerleon in the south, which maintained Roman law and order among the Demetae and the Silures. The former Silurian and Ordovician lands were administered by Roman officials, who saw to it that forts and fortlets were built at convenient intervals along the excellent roads that Roman engineers had made. Roman Britain as a whole was divided into two zones, the civil and the military, the former enjoying the amenities of the Roman way of life, the latter the attention of the Roman army.

Another strategic site on the Welsh borders was *Viroconium Cornoviorum*, now known as Wroxeter, 5 miles (8 km) to the east of Shrewsbury. It was the capital city of the Cornovii tribe and once the fourth largest city in Roman Britain after London, Cirencester and St Albans.

The settlement is entirely of Roman origin, probably beginning as a temporary marching camp established beside the great arterial route of Watling Street around 48 AD and would then have stood on the edge of the Roman Empire, forming part of its frontier with Wales. The discovery, in 1975, of a fortress on the site sheds some light on the likely next phase of the city's development. In AD 58, some ten years after the site had first been settled, the Emperor Nero decided to secure the Imperial boundary by subjugating the adjoining Welsh lands. This was to see the military presence in this key outpost change from a temporary campsite to a permanent garrison.

In its heyday, *Viroconium* was home to more than 6,000 inhabitants and has been described as one of the best examples of second century town planning. With the majority of its 200-acre site still awaiting excavation, *Viroconium* already boasts one of the largest surviving sections of Roman wall in Britain together with extensive remains of the city's baths and hypocaust, making it a uniquely important site.

Recent archaeological surveys have confirmed that early Welsh chieftains lived in the Roman ruins in the fifth and sixth centuries, after the Roman withdrawal. It became the headquarters of eastern Powys and it was probably rebuilt in timber after its decay. It is thought that it could be the 'Dre Wen' ('*white town*') lamented in early

1. *The Roman site at Wroxeter; 2. Caerleon barracks; 3. Segontium (at Caernarfon)*

Welsh poetry after it was destroyed and burnt by Mercian Saxons.

The whole of Wales lay in the military zone, save for the south-east corner, where a substantial civilian settlement was established to the east of Caerleon, halfway between modern Newport and Chepstow. This was *Venta Silurum*, Caerwent. Originally peopled in all probability by time-expired legionaries from Caerleon, Caer-went became the tribal capital of the Silures. It grew to be a splendid civilised place, with baths, shops and public buildings, probably second only in importance to Bath in the south-west of Britain. Caer-went was an oasis in a desert of military control, although there is archaeological evidence of the existence of three Roman villas near the south coast. One was at Llantwit Major, thought to have been built in the middle of the second century AD; the other two west of Cardiff, one a substantial farm and the other believed to have been concerned with the smelting of iron, also dating from the second century.

With these exceptions, civilian life in Roman Wales was limited to the settlements that grew up around the main forts, and to the communities engaged in mining, of which three examples will be given. Gold was mined in the area around Pumsaint, between Lampeter and Llandeilo (the Dolau Cothi mines); lead was worked in Roman times a few miles north-west of Wrexham in the north, while copper in considerable quantities was taken from Parys Mountain, inland from Amlwch in the north-eastern corner of Anglesey. It is possible that the mineral wealth of Wales was administered by civilians acting under military jurisdiction. Generally speaking, however, Wales was directly and sternly ruled by the Roman army, units of which, operating from their two great bases, would have patrolled the territory ceaselessly on their well-made roads.

A few sites will be briefly described here, either because they were of outstanding importance, such as Caerleon and Caer-went, or because they were remote like Tomen y Mur, or because their remains are now vestigial, as at *Segontium*.

Caerleon (340 907), possibly a contraction of *Castra Legionum*, the Camp

The amphitheatre at Caerleon

of the Legions, was certainly the most important Roman site in Wales, occupying more than 50 acres (20-23 ha). Today it is mostly built upon – for instance, the local parish church stands in the very middle of the Roman fort on the exact spot which was once adorned by the headquarters of the second Augusta legion. Enough, however, remains of this spectacular fort, built on the banks of the Usk, to give a strong impression to today's visitor of the might of Rome in the first century AD. Giraldus Cambrensis visited Caerleon at the end of the twelfth century and commented thus:

> immense places ... a lofty tower ... remarkable hot baths, the remains of temples and an amphitheatre ... wherever you look, you can see construction dug deep into the earth, conduits for water, underground passage and air-vents ...

The amphitheatre to which Giraldus refers was thoroughly excavated in the twentieth century; it stands well outside the fort and is immensely impressive. It is said to have seated 6,000 spectators; it was most likely used for military exercises and parades, though it cannot be ruled out that occasionally the hearts of off-duty soldiers were gladdened by the sight of gladiatorial combats. Some time in the middle of the third century, sixty or seventy years before the Roman Empire embraced Christianity, two Roman soldiers stationed in Caerleon were put to death for their Christian faith. These early martyrs were called Aaron and Julius; their martyrdom is confirmed by Giraldus, who added the information that in later years two churches in Caerleon were dedicated to their memory. A fourth-century pewter bowl that was dug up at Caer-went and is now on view in the museum at Newport, Gwent. It is the oldest surviving Christian artefact in Wales.

A Roman posting to *Segontium* (485 624) can hardly have been popular with the troops; it is situated half a mile (0.8 km) south of Caernarfon and 150 feet (45 m) above the shore in a bleak and exposed position. Segontium was at the end of the road. It was an auxiliary fort, built to accommodate 1,000 men, its purpose to maintain the Roman peace in Anglesey and in Llŷn. The original fort was put up by Agricola's men in 78 AD and covers 5.5 acres (2.22 ha); its wooden buildings were protected by a rampart 5 feet (1.5 m) high, on the top of which was fixed a wooden palisade. Surrounding the fort was a pair of ditches. This lonely Roman outpost was in use on and off throughout the occupation. There is no archaeological evidence that any provision was made for the entertainment or relaxation of Roman soldiers when off duty, unless the comfort afforded by religion may be placed in that category. In the little museum on the site is an altar to Minerva, dug up in the fort, and in 1959 a temple dedicated to Mithras was excavated. From Segontium a Roman road ran south to another auxiliary fort in an even lonelier situation, that of Tomen y Mur.

In the bleak moorland 5 miles (8 km) south of Ffestiniog and a mile (1.6 km) east of the former Trawsfynydd power station the patient and the painstaking student will find the traces of the most remote auxiliary fort in Roman Britain. Built on Agricola's orders shortly after 78 AD, Tomen y Mur (706 386) was linked by road with Segontium to the north-west, to

Caerhun to the north and to Brithdir to the south. The original fort was made of wood and turves, but when it was reduced in size some years later a stone wall marked the new rampart. Today the aeroplane sees more of the fort than does the walker, but even so the outlines are reasonably clear. Inside the fort is a mound whose purpose is puzzling until it is realised that the Normans passed that way 1,000 years later and chose the site of the west gate of the Roman fort for the erection of a motte and bailey, which is commemorated in the Welsh name Tomen y Mur (*tomen*: mound; *mur*: wall). Near the fort may be seen a flat area which had been artificially levelled to serve as a parade ground, and away to the north-east the remains of an amphitheatre are visible. Tomen y Mur is believed to have been the only auxiliary fort that was allowed the luxury of such an amenity, which surely shows that even the hardheaded Romans recognised the need for some compensation to be given to those soldiers unlucky enough to have been posted to that outpost.

The contrast today between a North Sea oil rig and a Cotswold village can hardly be greater than that between Tomen y Mur and Caer-went. Caer-went, or *Venta Silurum*, as the Romans knew it (469 905) is well worth a visit: in addition to being visually exciting, it reveals the other side of Roman occupation policy. It was as though the Romans wanted to show the conquered Silures the benefits to be derived from cooperating with them. *Venta Silurum* became not only the place which Roman soldiers wanted to visit when on leave from duties with the legion in Caerleon, but also the tribal capital of the

Tomen y Mur

Silures to which the leading men of the Silures were invited. Employment, houses and entertainment were all available for their use and enjoyment. The town covered 45 acres (18.21 ha) and offered most of the amenities of a small Romano-British town in the Civil Zone, public baths, a forum, shops and a small amphitheatre. The walls that surrounded the town still stand, in places reaching a height of 15 feet. The modern village of Caer-went, which is all part and parcel of *Venta Silurum*, enjoys an enviable position, pleasantly situated close to modern roads, but quite screened from them.

Roman withdrawal

The Romans withdrew from Wales shortly before the end of the fourth century AD; such a long period of occupation inevitably left its mark on the conquered population, even though Roman influence in Wales was considerably less than in the Civil Zone, further east in Britain. In Wales the most obvious proof of the Roman presence lay in the Latin words that crept into common Celtic usage, words to do with practical matters in which Roman soldiers excelled, to do with fighting and

building. Rather more tenuous was the effect Roman military might had in helping to unify those Celtic tribes who had had the courage to stand up against them. That in after years, when new threats to the Celtic homelands were forthcoming from other quarters, the Silures and the Ordovices were able to take the lead and organise resistance may at least in part be attributed to their earlier reputation

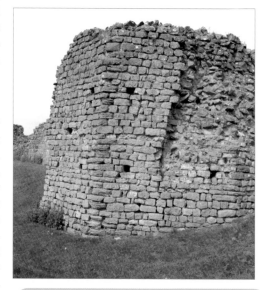

Caer-went

gained when they had dared to oppose the Roman invader.

Finally it must be put on record that Christianity first came to Wales in the ranks of Roman soldiers. Mention has already been made to two Roman soldiers dying for their Christian faith in Caerleon, but after Constantine, who had been proclaimed Emperor in York, accepted Christianity in about 314, Christianity became the leading religion in the empire, so that some knowledge of it in all probability will have been passed on to those Celts, who had contact with their Roman masters in various forts and mining settlements in Wales. Whether or not Christianity survived the Roman withdrawal from Wales at the end of that century will be considered in due course.

Roman remains
in the twentieth century
Eight places will be described here, stretching from Anglesey to the south coast of Glamorgan. The A5 ends its long journey in the town of Holyhead, above whose harbour can been seen the medieval parish church of St Cybi. This harbour was of considerable importance to the Romans as it afforded a safe anchorage for those Roman ships whose responsibility it was to patrol the Irish Sea. In addition the copper mined in north-eastern Anglesey will have been exported from Holyhead. By the beginning of the fourth century AD Roman occupation problems in Britain had begun to multiply as invaders threatened from several different directions. Hence from about 300 AD forts were constructed at many points along Britain's long and exposed shoreline. One was built at Holyhead on the headland, where now the church looks across the harbour. This fort, known as Caer Gybi (246 827), enclosed the land now occupied by the church and churchyard; it was only a small fort, hardly amounting to an acre (0.4 ha) in extent, but it gave adequate protection against possible invasion from the sea. Its surrounding wall may still be seen, rising in places to about 15 feet (4.57 m) in height; as the wall was 5 feet (1.52 m) thick, it is possible to walk with safety along the rampart. Of its four original round corner towers, three have survived.

Caerhun (776 704), built in the early years of the Roman occupation of Wales as a staging post on the road from Chester (*Deva*) to Caernarfon (*Segontium*), stood near the river Conwy 4½ miles (7.24 km) up the river from Conwy. The traveller today, moving south from Conwy on the B5106, in search of what remains of *Canovium*, should make for the parish church because the walls of the churchyard are supported by a Roman rampart. Little remains today beyond the outlines of the walls, which are very clear on the south side of the fort. Nevertheless, thanks to a thorough excavation in the 1920s, the story of the fort has been revealed. It is thought to have been built of wood in 75 AD and rebuilt in stone about 70 years later; the site of the fort seems to have been chosen with a view to defending the Roman position from any attack from the river, proof of which has been furnished by the discovery of traces of a jetty and a dock. The Roman occupation of *Canovium* went on until the fourth century, though most of the buildings are believed to have been destroyed in about the year 200.

A short stop 4 miles (6.43 km) west of Bala on the A494 road to Dolgellau that runs alongside the lake will reveal, on a spur to the north of the road the ramparts of a small Roman fort. Caer Gai (877 315) is to be found half a mile (0.8 km) north-east of the village of Llanuwchllyn. Only the ramparts on the south-west and south-east sides of the fort are well-preserved, though an entrance gap on the south-west side is also clearly recognisable as such. All the land encompassed by the fort has been completely filled in. During the excavation of the site a shrine dedicated to Hercules was unearthed near the north-east gate, its inscription, now in the safe keeping of the National Museum of Wales in Cardiff, indicating that a cavalry regiment from the north of Gaul had been stationed at Caer Gai, which, it appears, was only in Roman occupation from about 78 to 130 AD.

Holidaymakers, based on Llandrindod Wells in central Wales, who want to take a break from playing golf or bowls, fishing, or taking the foul-smelling (though doubtless health-giving!) waters, could do worse than make a short excursion to Castell Collen (055 628), which lies a mile (1.6 km) or so to the north of the spa, off A4081. This large fort was built on high ground between the river Ithon and one of the streams that feed it. As a result of two excavations, one before the First World War, the other after the Second, it is thought that the original fort, a wooden affair, was built between 75 and 78 AD; it covered a large area of about 5 acres (2 ha) and provided accommodation for about 1,000 men. It was bounded by a ditch and a wall of turves which was later strengthened by the addition of stones. At the beginning of the third century the area of the fort was halved, the north-west part being abandoned; the strength of the garrison was reduced to 500 men, but the most important of the new buildings were made of stone. Vestigial remains of these stone buildings, more particularly those of the Commandant's house and the headquarters building, have survived, but all traces of the wooden barracks in which the soldiers were housed have long since disappeared. It should be stressed that this excursion is really only for the connoisseur as there is little to be seen, though much to be learned from the geographical location and from the finds which are on view in the museum in Temple Street, Llandrindod Wells.

An hour's drive separates Castell Collen from Brecon Gaer, which lies 4 miles (6.43 km) west of Brecon, off the A40, high up above the road, on a strategically important site. The Gaer (002

Roman shops foundations at Caer-went

297), a cavalry fort with accommodation for 500 horsemen, was built in this key position about 80 AD, when the newly-conquered Celtic lands needed to be consolidated. Like other forts it originally consisted of wooden buildings, protected by earthen ramparts, which gave place to stone when they were rebuilt in the following century. There is much more to be seen here than in the forts already described; the site was excavated by Sir Mortimer Wheeler in the 1920s.

Today there are on three sides of the fort large sections of well-constructed walls, still in position, rising up to about 10 feet (3 m) in height (the north side has been incorporated in a farm). Three gateways remain, of which the southern one is particularly well-preserved with substantial parts of the guardroom walls still standing both sides of the gate. An unusual feature in the Gaer was the presence inside the fort of a bath-house, which normally was built outside the walls. Also of interest is the fact that there is strong evidence that there was a large civilian settlement established outside the north gate. The Gaer was continuously occupied until about 200, when it appears to have been evacuated only to be brought back into use again 100 years later.

Eight miles (12.87 km) west of the Gaer, on the old Roman road that runs from Trecastle to Llandovery, are to be found vestigial remains of two marching camps. There is little to be seen here except earthen ramparts and ditches, but to the inner eye of imagination these so-called marching camps (of which there are sixteen surviving sites in Wales and the Marches) make a strong appeal because these camps date from the very earliest years of Roman campaigning against the Celtic lands. Most of these camps were abandoned even before the year 80 AD, by which time organised opposition to the advance of Roman arms had come to an end. Here at Y Pigwyn (828 313) were two such camps, the smaller of the two being built a few years later than the larger one, within the same perimeter. A whole legion with its auxiliary troops could be quartered there, but only for a short time, indeed sometimes for only one night. They were transit camps with a difference, as the front-line troops may have been

1. Caerhun wall above Conwy river ; 2. Roman slates, Llwydfaen ; 3. & 4. Dolau Cothi gold mine

detailed, immediately on arrival, to dig themselves adequate defences for protection for the ensuing night. Stoutly-built forts in later years, like that at the Gaer, were made possible only by the successful efforts of these units of Roman infantry, who made good use of the Spartan facilities afforded by Y Pigwyn and other such marching camps.

Halfway along the A482, which runs in a south-easterly direction from Lampeter towards Llandovery, is the strangely-named village of Pumsaint (the five saints referred to in the name were, according to tradition, quintuplets, all of whom became holy men). Half a mile (0.8 km) from here the Romans mined gold at Dolau Cothi (665 405). The Dolau Cothi Gold Mines visitor centre is now operated by the National Trust; you can find out more from their website: http://www.nationaltrust.org.uk/dolaucothi-gold-mines

The precious metal was obtained partly by opencast methods and partly by tunnelling into shallow galleries – the entrances to some of these tunnels are still clearly visible but, as mining has gone on in the neighbourhood on a number of occasions since Roman times, local enquiries are recommended; caution is also stressed as some of the galleries are too dangerous to explore. Excavation in recent years has greatly increased our knowledge of Roman mining methods here; for instance, traces have been discovered of an aqueduct running up-country for more than 10 miles (16 km), providing water which is essential for smelting. On display in the National Museum in Cardiff is part of a Roman water-wheel taken from this economically important site, which, though organised by civilian engineers, was certainly supervised and controlled by units of the Roman army.

The Romans came and settled along the coast of south Glamorgan, developing over the years a large complex of farm buildings, based on a villa, erected in about 150. The original farm, built in wood, probably consisted of domestic structures built round two sides of a double courtyard, complete with the full array of bath-houses that the Romans always insisted on. To this were later added many barns and workshops. In about 300 there was a wholesale rebuilding of the farm in

1. Roman wall at Caer Gybi, Holyhead ;
2. & 3. Roman Museum, Caerleon

stone; in this transformation four mosaic floors were laid and several rooms were decorated with painted plaster. Halfway through this fourth century a barbarian raid, presumably from the sea, took place which wrought great havoc in the villa, in one part of which archaeologists discovered the mangled skeletons of many men and horses. Whether the farm continued to function after this disaster is open to doubt. It is necessary here briefly to anticipate events to be dealt with later in the book, because tradition has it that Illtud, one of the founding fathers of Christianity in Wales, landed hereabouts from Brittany towards the end of the fifth century and actually lived in the Roman villa, at the same time giving his name to the place, Llanilltud, later to be corrupted to Llantwit. Whether or not there is any truth underlying this tradition, it is certain that there was only a short lapse of time between the end of the Roman occupation of the district and early Christian settlement.

Between Llantwit Major and Cardiff evidence has accumulated of two further Roman villas: excavation at one of the sites, at Whitton (081 713) revealed traces of Roman farm buildings, erected on an Iron Age settlement, while the other villa, which is much nearer Cardiff, at Ely (147 762) is thought to have concerned itself with the smelting of iron. On into the centre of Cardiff, is where the mighty castle looms up, a massive structure, mostly rebuilt in the nineteenth century, but securely based on Roman foundations. Round the corner from the castle in the splendid array of civic buildings stands out the National Museum of Wales, which is rightly renowned for its collection of prehistoric, Roman and early Christian exhibits, along with artefacts from later periods. The other Roman museums in Wales are virtually site museums, as at Caerleon, Newport (for Caer-went), Brecon (Y Gaer), Llandrindod Wells (for Castell Collen), and Caernarfon (*Segontium*).

An aerial view of Caer-went – the best preserved town of Roman Britain

The Celtic Church

The Age of the Saints and Germanic attacks

At the beginning of the fifth century in Britain, the clock was well and truly put back; the Celts, who inhabited all southern Britain, were left by the departing Roman armies to fend for themselves. Before long, unarmed, untrained and unprotected, they had to face up to attacks from many quarters, from Jutes and Angles and Saxons, and from Picts and Scots. Very little is known for certain about these dark and dismal days of transition in the fifth century and what little we do know is mostly derived from the sole surviving contemporary source, Gildas, a monk, who had been educated at Llantwit Major, of which distinguished seminary more will be said later. As Gildas died in the second half of the sixth century, what he wrote down must either have been hearsay or the recollections of men who in their old age reminisced for the benefit of the young monk from Wales. From Gildas' book *The Downfall of Britain* it would be safer to gather impressions rather than facts. Out of the thick mist that obscured most of this fifth century there occasionally appeared in outline the dim figure of Vortigern, who made himself leader of the Celts. Much has been written about him, but little is known beyond the fact that in the middle of the century he invited Angle and Saxon mercenaries from across the North Sea to come to Britain in order to help him to defend his lands, probably against the Picts. Hengist and Horsa, the Anglo-Saxon leaders, accepted the invitation, rendered the necessary assistance, and elected to stay on, and so renewed the foreign occupation of Britain. Of the one and only Arthur, whose adventures were set in this same century, nothing factual may be recounted. Gildas, not the most reliable of chroniclers, failed to mention him, either through ignorance of his existence or, as one tradition insists, because Arthur had killed his brother.

But there is enough evidence in Welsh literature and folklore to be certain that King Arthur unified the southern Celtic tribes of Britain – by then, Cumbric, Welsh and Cornish-speaking – and was victorious in many battles against the Germanic

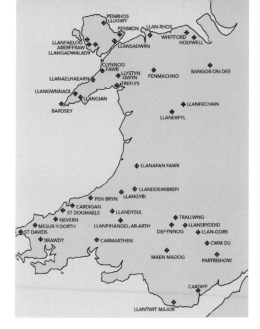

All the same there was a grim struggle going on in Wales for survival at this time when there was no central authority. The most significant development occurred when there came down from Strathclyde, in southern Scotland, a Romanised Celt called Cunedda, who in the early years of this fifth century settled in Anglesey, from which island he drove out Irish immigrants who had lived there for several decades. This Christian Cunedda ruled from Aberffraw on the west coast of Anglesey and there founded a dynasty whose descendants were to serve Wales faithfully and well for more than 800 years.

While it is true that there is no proof that Christianity survived in Wales after the withdrawal of the Romans, the fifth century (despite the darkness that fell upon the rest of Britain, which reverted to paganism) witnessed the rapid spread of Christianity in the far west. Nevertheless it is as well to regard this as the return of Christianity to Wales rather than to see it as surviving from Roman days. Had Christianity really managed to hang on after the Romans' departure, then surely traces of it would have been found in the south-east of the country, where it was

tribes of the eastern shores, curbing their advance and securing a fifty-year peace.

By the year 500 most of Britain was in a state of turmoil and disarray, with Angles, Saxons, Jutes and the men from the north challenging the Celtic Britons for a share in the overlordship of the country. Wales alone at this time stood as yet unmolested by these invaders, and indeed earned the distinction of being the only part of the former Roman Empire in the west to escape capture by marauders.

1. & 2. St Illtud's church, Llanilltud Fawr;
2. Standing stones, Cwm Gwaun's churchyard

known to have been practised by the Romans; whereas in fact the record does not bear this out.

While many countries on Continental Europe and eastern Britain suffered what is called 'the Dark Ages', the same cannot be said of Wales and the Celtic lands of the western seas. Here Christianity thrives, churches and monasteries and centres of learning were established and early Welsh literature flourished.

The first missionaries

The surprisingly speedy expansion of Christianity in Wales in the fifth century, at a time when it was abandoned altogether further east in Britain, was above all due to energetic Celtic missionaries coming by sea from western parts of Gaul, probably Brittany. The greatest authority on early Christian tombstones in Wales, Dr Nash-Williams, draws our attention to the fact that the earliest memorial stones were all inscribed in exactly the same way as those found in western Gaul. He further noted that while there are many of these remarkable Christian memorial stones in Wales, there are none in the south-east, which was the centre of Christianity when the Romans ruled from Caerleon. In addition to these Christian missionaries sailing along the western sea-routes, Irish Christians were at the same time settling in Anglesey and in coastal areas of Wales further south. The archaeological proof of this Irish colonisation is strong, because the Irish Christians had devised a special kind of script for their memorial inscriptions, known as Ogham. Of the very many memorial inscriptions of the fifth and sixth centuries that still survive in Wales, some are in Latin, some are in Ogham, and fortunately some are in both. Such a stone, still to be seen in the nave of the church at Nevern, in Pembrokeshire, which carries both scripts, enabled scholars to decipher the secrets of Ogham, which consists of a series of notches cut into the edges of the memorial stones; there are several of these fascinating stones, bearing both scripts, on exhibition at the National Museum of Wales in Cardiff. Details of these Christian memorial stones, which are still in situ, will be given in a later section.

A third possible factor which may have helped the development of Christianity in Wales was the immigration in the early years of the fifth century of Christian refugees from areas further east in Britain, who sought the security of the Welsh hills when the withdrawal of the Roman army left them unprotected. In addition there is good reason to believe that close contact was established between the Celtic immigrants from Gaul and the colonists from Ireland, communication between the various parts of Wales being facilitated by the excellent Roman roads. This cultural contact, which could have helped in later years to unify the Welsh, was fractured when Cunedda and his successors extended their rule from Anglesey to north and central Wales, to the extreme discomfiture of the Irish settlers. It was into this Wales that there came towards the end of this confused fifth century an outstanding Christian missionary, Illtud.

i) Illtud

When considering these early Christian missionaries it has to be stressed that hard facts are difficult to come by; little was written down for many centuries, and when eventually learned monks put on record what they had heard, wishful thinking has to be allowed for. Nevertheless Illtud was certainly one of the founding fathers of the Christian church in Wales. It seems very likely that he hailed from Brittany, from whence he sailed to south Wales towards the end of the fifth century, landing on the south coast of Glamorgan at a spot south of the modern Cowbridge, a spot which had previously been inhabited both by men of the Iron Age and by the Romans. A mile (1.6 km) from there Illtud established a monastic college which in the course of time achieved an outstanding reputation for scholarship. This place is now known as Llantwit Major. From this centre of devotion and learning men went forth spiritually and intellectually equipped to spread Christianity and to establish the monastic movement in Wales.

A suitable site would be chosen and a wooden cross set up by the missionary monk who then built himself a simple hut. If he succeeded in attracting an audience and keeping it, he would enclose the area with a circular bank of earth. This was the first *llan*, an area set apart for religious purposes. Sometimes these monks actually settled on sites already enclosed by stone walls, the remains of Bronze Age barrows. All this started in the early days of the sixth century at a time when Illtud himself chose to live the life of a hermit, first at Oystermouth on Gower, and later at Llanhamlach in the Upper Usk valley.

According to Giraldus Cambrensis, writing more than 600 years later, the mare that carried provisions to Illtud in his rural retreat at Llanhamlach:

> became gravid after being covered by a stag and gave birth to a creature which could run very fast, its front part being like that of a horse and its haunches resembling those of a deer.

Today in this same parish of Llanhamlach, 4 miles (6.43 km) south-east of Brecon, will be found on private ground belonging to Manest Farm, a Neolithic long barrow, with the anachronistic name of Tŷ Illtud, the House of Illtud. It appears that anything old was thought to have something to do with this remarkable man. An added curiosity is that on the walls of the forecourt of the tomb there are carvings, which are certainly much later in date than the tomb itself, some of which look remarkably like crosses as though the eager early Christians believed that by scratching crosses on a pagan tomb some sort of posthumous respectability might be conferred upon the dead. Illtud's presence in this part of Wales was clearly felt, as indeed it was also felt further north on the banks of the Mawddach, above Dolgellau. Tradition has it that Illtud chose this remote region for an early *llan*, which only in later centuries became the spiritual centre of a village, which bore his name, Llanelltud. In Illtud's *llan* were later erected in a circular churchyard a succession of churches, which the Cistercian monks from nearby Cymer Abbey served until its dissolution in the sixteenth century. It is interesting to note that Illtud had a brother, who was also a priest, whose inscribed tombstone has survived. It is now to be seen in the church of the village named after him, Llansadwrn, in Anglesey, 4 miles (6.43 km) west of Beaumaris.

The scene changes to central Wales, where in the Brecon Beacons to the south-west of Brecon there is a patch of hilly moorland that bears his name, Mynydd Illtud. Here at a height of 1,100 feet (335 m), a short distance from the National Park Visitor Centre (Mountain Centre) at Libanus, is a circular churchyard (the church is Victorian) in which, according to tradition, Illtud lies buried. Half a mile (0.8 km) to the east of the churchyard is a Bronze Age burial cairn, which the reader will hardly be surprised to learn is known as Bedd Illtyd, Illtud's grave! Wherever he was buried, he is thought to have died in 540, the doyen of the missionary movement. As scholar and Christian leader he was outstanding; his great memorial was the seminary he set up at Llantwit Major, which became famous as a centre of learning, where, along with the knowledge of Christianity, were inculcated the classics, grammar, rhetoric and philosophy.

ii) Cadog and Dyfrig
Another famous missionary, though of a lesser magnitude than Illtud, whose contemporary and fellow-worker in the field he was, was Cadog; he was the son of Gwynllyw, a very powerful figure in south-east Wales in the early sixth century and something of a villain too, whom Cadog is credited with having converted to Christianity somewhat late in life. So devoted, however, did his father become to the Christian cause that the cathedral at Newport was dedicated to him under

the later Anglo-Norman form of his name, Woolos. The son, whose floruit was in the early years of the sixth century (though his actual dates are unknown), set up a seat of learning in south Glamorgan, at Llancarfan, which is only about 5 miles (8 km) east of Illtud's seminary at Llantwit Major. Unfortunately, the actual position of Cadog's school of learning has remained undiscovered, prompting the likely theory that today's church stands on its very site. That it achieved a great reputation for its scholarship cannot be gainsaid, especially, it seems, in the study of the Classics. Cadog above all became a great authority on the Roman poet Virgil, perhaps fittingly insofar as the astonishing claim was made on his behalf that he was a descendant of Virgil's master, Augustus himself, the first Emperor of Rome! One of the curious scraps of information that have been handed down about Cadog is that every spring he spent Lent on the island of Steep Holm in the Bristol Channel, to which island Gildas also retreated when he wrote his history on *The Downfall of Britain*. Cadog's fame must have spread far and wide because there are churches dedicated to him not only in south-west, south-east Wales and in Anglesey, but also in Scotland, Cornwall and in distant Brittany.

Rather later than Cadog, but still in the sixth century, lived a missionary variously known as Dyfrig, Dubricius and Devereux; there is a village in Herefordshire near Kilpeck, named St Devereux, whose parish church is dedicated to St Dubricius! He lived and worked in south-eastern Wales and over the borders in what is now Herefordshire. The various references to the holy man's life and career suggest the existence of a thin dividing line between fact and fiction. That he actually lived is certain (he founded a monastery in Herefordshire); that he did half the things attributed to him by Geoffrey of Monmouth most unlikely. In this category must be placed Geoffrey's assertion that he crowned King Arthur! Of his status as a Christian missionary, however, there can be no doubt. He wandered about the country far less than most missionary monks at that time, although there are strong associations with him on Caldey Island; and, when he died in 612, he was considered to be of sufficient consequence

Old 'llans': 1. Ysbyty Cynfyn, Ceredigion; 2. Llangelynnin, Conwy valley

to be buried in Bardsey Island, from which resting place his bones were removed 500 years later and transferred to Llandaf, presumably because of the strength of the legend that he had caused the building of the first cathedral in that place.

iii) St David

In the south-west of the country there were three monks in the sixth century whose missionary endeavours stood out. Far and away the greatest was St David himself, the other two being Teilo and Padarn. Indeed Teilo and Padarn accompanied St David on a pilgrimage to Rome and Jerusalem. All the sixth- and seventh-century missionaries are referred to as saints, but in fact all save David were honorary saints, as only David was canonised by the church authorities in Rome. Of Teilo's life and achievements only a skeleton outline is possible. He is believed to have founded a monastery at Llandeilo in Carmarthenshire, and he is credited with having been the third Bishop of St David's; certainly there are many churches in Wales dedicated to him. There is a curious story in circulation that Teilo's skull was the private property of a well-known family in the Llandeilo district. Until about fifty years ago, so the story goes, pilgrims to that house were offered a drink of water from the skull, in the belief that such water possessed curative properties. Of St Padarn (or Paternus) even less is known than of Teilo. He was born in Wales and spent his life in the south-west and west of the country, founding a monastery which in after years acquired a great reputation at Llanbadarn Fawr, which today is almost a part of Aberystwyth. Though many churches were dedicated to him, he, like his contemporary Teilo, lived in the shadow of St David.

Most famous old churches occupy prominent positions in the landscape where all may see and wonder, but it is not so with the cathedral at St David's. Uninformed visitors, having parked their cars, may at first look about them in vain for the 'house of David', Tyddewi, until they are directed to the steep slope below whose thirty-nine steps may be seen the cathedral, and the splendid remains of the Bishop's Palace. It was down here where three cathedrals have since stood that David founded his monastery. It is ironical that so little firm facts are known about one whose fame is so great. The

1. St Non's Chapel; 2. St David's Cathedral

explanation seems to be that more than 500 years were allowed to elapse before his life was written about, and even then the motives of the writer may well have been mixed. When Rhigyfarch (the son of a Bishop of St David's) set about, at the end of the eleventh century, putting on record the life and achievements of St David, the Norman penetration into southern parts of Wales had become so deep that the continued independence of St David's from the authority of Canterbury was thought to be at risk.

Hence it was essential, if Wales was to withstand the Norman pressure, that the greatness of the father of Welsh Christianity had to be emphasised and embellished with every anecdote and legend that the intervening years had provided.

This south-western corner of Wales must have furnished the young David with much food for thought, as he saw around him so much evidence of earlier human occupation. Tradition has assigned his birth to a cave less than a mile south of modern St David's, where may still be seen the ruins of an early church dedicated to his mother Nonna, who is reputed to have given birth to her illustrious son on that very site. Nearby is an ancient well now dedicated to St Mary, and in the field in which the little church stands are several stones still in position that speak of an earlier prehistoric settlement.

St David is believed to have been educated at a monastic establishment at Henfynyw, near Aberaeron in Ceredigion, before going back to the land of his birth, where he founded a monastery at Glyn Rhosyn, where St David's Cathedral now stands. It is incorrect to refer to him as Archbishop of St David's, or even as Bishop, because there was as yet no see and no diocese. David all his adult life was abbot of his monastery, which, despite the lack of stress laid there on scholarship, became even more famous than Illtud's. Here David made his mark, as an ascetic Christian, of gentle disposition, a firm disciplinarian, an able organiser, and above all an inspired and persuasive preacher. It is the stuff of legend, true or false, that he drank nothing but water and harnessed his monks to the plough; despite this or because of it, disciples flocked to the monastery.

The stories about him are legion: one concerns an address he is supposed to have given, when a young man, to a synod convened in a remote place in Ceredigion, now named after him, Llanddewibrefi. It was said that when David was called upon to speak he did so with such fire and passion that the very ground on which he stood rose up under his feet so that he found himself standing on a mound, proving to the congregation, now grouped below him, that he should be recognised as their leader. The story may be apocryphal, but that it should have been invented clearly revealed the need felt to justify the way David stood out above his fellow-men.

He died at a great age on March 1st 588; Jan Morris in *The Matter of Wales* quotes his biographer Rhigyfarch as saying that David's last sermon, preached shortly before he died, contained these words:

> Lords, brothers and sisters, rejoice and hold fast your faith and belief and do the little things that you have heard from and seen in me.

1. Penmon priory; 2. St Trillo's stone chapel

Jan Morris added:

> A great host of angels filled the town and all manner of delectable music was heard and the sun shone brilliantly, and Jesus Christ took into himself the soul of David the Saint with great pomp and honour.

Fifty Welsh churches have since been dedicated to him, although none of them is to be found in northern Wales. He was canonised in 1120 and thereafter became the patron saint of Wales, the anniversary of his death on the first of March becoming the National Day. The church authorities in Rome, moreover, subsequently decreed that two pilgrimages to St David's should rate as highly as one to Rome itself.

iv) Beuno

All the Celtic saints so far referred to hailed either from south Wales or from Brittany; the last one to be mentioned, however, Beuno, belonged to the north, in which area his contribution was equal in importance to that of David himself in the south. Although some authorities think that he was educated in Gwent, he was born towards the end of the sixth century at Berriew, a few miles south of Welshpool, where he spent most of his early years as a monk. A mile (1.6 km) from today's picturesque black and white village of Berriew is a Bronze Age standing stone, proudly referred to as Maen Beuno, Beuno's Stone; once again our forebears sought to make an emblem of their pagan past respectable by giving it a Christian connotation. This stone was said to have been the saint's first pulpit.

Exasperated, it is believed, by the proximity of the hated Saxons across the Severn, Beuno moved north-west further into Wales, finally settling in Llŷn at Clynnog Fawr, where he received from one of Cunedda's successors a piece of land on which he built a monastery. This monastery was to last for over 300 years until it was destroyed in a Viking raid. Nearby Beuno consecrated to Christian use an ancient prehistoric well to which in after years generations of local people had recourse when they sought alleviation from their various ailments. For centuries it became the custom for the sick, after being bathed in the well, to be carried back to the churchyard where they were placed on a pile of straw strewn on the saint's tomb, it being fervently believed that a night spent in this wise would guarantee restoration to full health.

Inside today's church, a relatively modern building, dating from the fifteenth century, and built on the site of Beuno's seventh-century monastery, is a huge chest, known inevitably as the Chest of Beuno, though undoubtedly medieval. Lambs or calves born with a certain distinguishing mark on their ears were considered the special concern of Beuno; their owners were required to come to the churchyard with their calves and lambs the following Trinity Sunday when they had to pay a fee to their abbot because of the *Nod Beuno* (Beuno's mark) found on their livestock. This money, tradition insisted, was then placed in the chest, which perhaps, not surprisingly, was believed to possess miraculous powers. This custom was observed well into the nineteenth century.

Beuno, it seems, was as potent a force on sea as he was on land. A rock a mile (1.6 km) off-shore is still marked on the Ordnance Survey map as Gored Beuno; from this outcrop Beuno was reputed to bless the fishermen. He was also credited with the ability to walk on water. On one occasion, when returning from a visit to Anglesey, to his great regret he dropped into the sea a book of sermons he was reading. However, when he stepped on to dry land near Clynnog, to his great delight he saw his precious book set out to dry on a stone, where it was being guarded by a curlew. The grateful abbot proceeded to bless the curlew, which is why, it is fondly believed by some, it is still so difficult to find a curlew's nest!

When he died in 642, he was buried in his cell over which in time a chapel was erected, still known as Beuno's Chapel,

St Winifrede's well, Holywell

which is linked to the tower of St Beuno's Church by a stone-roofed passage. Of all the many legends that have crystallised around the name of Beuno, perhaps the best known, as well as being the most bizarre, concerned the strange adventure that befell his niece, Winifrede, who in her youth was one day waylaid. As she stoutly and successfully resisted the threatened rape, her frustrated attacker drew his sword and cut off her head. St Winifrede's Well at Holywell marks the spot where her severed head as it touched the ground, caused a great spring of water to gush forth. Happily her revered uncle miraculously appeared and restored the head to Winifrede's torso, thus enabling her for many years thereafter to serve the church as Abbess of Gwytherin. Many indeed are the churches in northern Wales dedicated to Beuno, especially in Llŷn and in Anglesey. Rightly is he regarded as the patron saint of northern Wales.

Christian wells and memorial stones

Throughout the fifth and sixth centuries Christian monks like David, Illtud, Cadog, Dyfrig, Padarn and Beuno, and a host of lesser-known missionaries, between them succeeded in Christianising most of Wales – at a time, be it remembered, when the rest of southern Britain had reverted to pagan ways. In all simple societies water supplies were of prime importance; as prehistoric settlement was widespread in Wales, a great many sources of water had been discovered. Early men generally came to identify springs and wells with the supernatural beings, which were believed to live in the water. Hence small offerings were dropped into the wells to ensure a continuing supply of water from the placated deities. Christian missionaries when they found old wells, tended to sanctify them and then turn them into healing wells, which were often associated with the same saints to whom the nearest churches were dedicated. Pagan Celtic peasants who, it is presumed, had always made their offerings to the wells, were after conversion encouraged to continue the practice, especially when their ailments were sometimes seen to disappear after treatment in the wells, where, after Christian sanctification, prayers were offered and blessings pronounced.

1. The Caldey stone; 2. The Llanspyddid stone

Francis Jones, in his authoritative *The Holy Wells of Wales*, cites over 100 examples of pre-Christian wells in the neighbourhood of which Christian churches were built. Such wells then received Christian dedications. This Christian well-cult, which must have helped greatly in winning over the pagan Celts to Christianity, was often associated too with pagan, prehistoric burial places. Seeing that prehistoric men chose to settle on sites near convenient water supplies, many a ruined cromlech and barrow were still visible often in the vicinity of wells in the fifth and sixth centuries. Over sixty instances are known in Wales of prehistoric megaliths being found near sanctified pre-Christian wells; these too were often sanctified by early Celtic missionaries, so that these prehistoric stones could also become a part of the healing process emanating from the holy wells.

Instances of this conversion to Christian use of prehistoric monuments may be seen at St Non's Chapel, near St David's, where the chapel ruins stand in a prehistoric stone circle, close to a pre-Christian well, now the Holy Well of St Mary; at Nevern, further north up the same coast, where near the church is a well, Ffynnon Garreg, sited near a prehistoric mound, Bedd Samson; at Llangybi, between Lampeter and Tregaron, near whose parish church is a well, Ffynnon Gybi, not far from Llech Gybi, a cromlech, where the sick used to

Llanbadarn stone

be taken to sleep after being dipped in the healing well. Finally at Llanfechain, north-west of Welshpool, in the round churchyard that surrounds St Garmon's Church is a Bronze Age mound, known as Garmon's Mound, 300 yards (275 m) from which is St Garmon's Well. All in all, during the rightly-named Age of the Saints, the Christian church took over lock, stock and barrel the outstanding features of those pre-Christian religious ceremonies that had to do with wells and megaliths.

Besides a remote track high up in the Brecon Beacons; in the garden of a private house in Llŷn; built into a farmyard wall near the road from Pwllheli to Caernarfon; in the middle of a field above the sea north of Cardigan, and in churches and churchyards the length and breadth of Wales will be found the gravestones of early Christians, converted by these Celtic missionaries in the fifth, sixth and early seventh centuries. In all, well over 100 such monuments have survived; the inscriptions, either in Latin or in Ogham, or in both, generally consist of the name of the dead person and of his or her father; sometimes an inscription is preceded by *HIC IACIT*, the more grammatical *HIC IACET* being rare, and often the words *IN PACE* have been added. Many stones also have carved on them some form of the Christian cross. The Chi-Rho monogram, that rarest of all Christian emblems, occurs twice on Welsh tombstones; both were dug up outside, but are now propped up inside the churches of Treflys in the parish of Cricieth, and Penmachno in Conwy.

The historic meeting at Aust
Nine years after St David, his great work done, had passed from the scene, the Pope sent to Britain in 597 St Augustine and a party of forty monks, who were charged with the onerous task of converting the Saxon heathen. As the newly-arrived missionaries struggled, not without a measure of success, to overcome the stubborn paganism of the Saxons, they must have been surprised to learn of the strength of the Christian church among the Celts in the west. At any rate in 602 Augustine sought a meeting with representatives of the Celtic Christians. Although he had been commissioned by the Pope to act in a friendly manner towards the Celts and to cooperate with them, he was perturbed to hear that in the

two centuries that had elapsed since direct control between Rome and Britain had ceased, practices in this Celtic church had deviated in certain respects from those current in Rome. The main differences were said to concern baptismal rites and the date set aside for the celebration of Easter, though in all probability Augustine may well have been offended by the affront to his authority implicit in the independent attitude of the Celtic Christians.

Our knowledge of what actually went on at this historic meeting between Augustine and the leaders of the Celts relies entirely on the account given by Bede, who lived nearly a century later and who was very much biased against the Celtic Christians, whom he regarded as the enemies of his church. The parties met at Aust, where the Romans before them had established a ferry, south of the Bristol Channel, opposite Chepstow. Augustine apparently expressed the hope that there would be full cooperation between the Celtic church and the newly-established church in Canterbury, but that to facilitate this, the Celts would have to abandon those practices that differed from existing Roman ones. The Celts listened and then asked for an adjournment to enable them to consult those who had sent them. The Celtic emissaries thereupon returned to their base, which was the great monastery at Bangor-on-Dee, south-east of modern Wrexham. Here, where no fewer than 2,400 monks were housed, they were advised after due discussion and debate to return to Aust and to accept Augustine's proposals on condition that he should behave towards them in what they regarded as a considerate manner, evidence of which would surely be demonstrated if the great man rose to receive them on their approach.

Augustine, little sensing the delicacy of the situation, remained seated and proceeded to repeat his demands concerning baptism and the timing of Easter in such hectoring tones that it became obvious to the Celts that no compromise was possible. Without such full agreement Augustine made it clear that no common effort to convert the pagan Saxons could be attempted. The opportunity passed; the Celts in anger refused the offer, and in return Augustine ominously threatened that if they would

Ffynnon Gybi – the well of St Cybi

not be his friends, they would have to take the consequences of being his enemies. The blood-stained sequel to this threat will be described later, but, as a result of this ill-starred conference, the rift between the two branches of the Christian church in Britain gaped ever wider.

Surviving Christian memorial stones and wells

This section will be a long one, for the most fortunate reason that Wales is blessed with an exceptionally rich heritage of reminders of the early days of Christianity. Most of the Christian memorial stones mentioned here commemorate the lives of Christians who died before Augustine brought back Christianity to the eastern parts of Britain at the end of the sixth century. A tribute must first be paid to the enthusiasm, the thoroughness and the scholarship of Dr V. E. Nash-Williams, whose book *The Early Christian Monuments of Wales*, published by the University of Wales in 1954, gives a detailed account of all the fifth- and early sixth-century Christian memorial stones that survived in Wales at the time of writing his book. This invaluable work of reference described every Christian burial stone that bore either an inscription (in Latin or in Ogham or in both) or an incised cross of varying designs. Only a selection of them will be included, either because the author has not visited them all; or because some of them in the intervening years have either deteriorated to such an extent that the inscriptions are no longer legible or have altogether disappeared; or because, in a small minority of cases, some have passed into the careful custodianship of right-minded private individuals, whose anonymity it seems prudent to protect, except in special circumstances.

Rarest of all early Christian monuments in Britain are those that bear, in addition to a Latin inscription, the Chi-Rho symbol, that is the combined first two letters of Christ in Greek, the Chi and the Rho, the Ch and the R. There are twelve in all in Britain, of which two are to be seen in northern Wales, one at Treflys, the other at Penmachno. Only the most committed enthusiasts will find their way to Treflys Church (532 379) which stands alone high up above the Black Rock sands on the south coast of Llŷn. To acquire the

One of the Penmachno stones

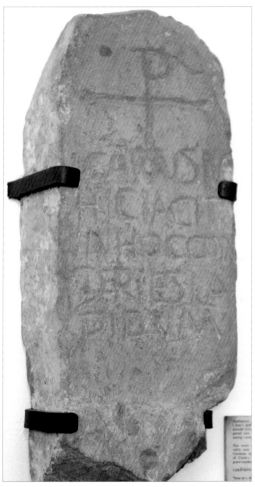

key to this church, which is always locked, and necessarily so, recourse has to be had to the rectory in Cricieth, which is 5 miles (8 km) away up narrow and tortuous country lanes. The inscribed stone, which was discovered in the churchyard, has found a home inside the church, where it stands against the north wall of the chancel. The actual Chi-Rho is of a transitional type, being halfway between a Chi-Rho proper and a cross; the accompanying inscription indicates that Jaconus, the son of Minus, was buried there.

Penmachno is a large village, situated on the B4406, about 3 miles (4.8 km) south-west of the A5 from which it branches off between Betws-y-coed and Pentrefoelas. The village church has provided sanctuary for four inscribed stones, all belonging to the fifth or early sixth centuries. The key is readily available from an address listed in the porch. The stone with the Chi-Rho monogram announces, in very imperfect Latin: 'Carausius lies here in the pile of stones'. This is no longer true, as all four stones were taken into the church from various sites outside, one of which was the garden wall of the Eagle Hotel, opposite the church, from which it was rescued in 1915! The accompanying photograph gives a good idea of this splendid early Christian monument. Of the other three stones in the church, one, with only a fragment of Latin inscription surviving, was dug up when the previous church was pulled down; another, still having intact five lines of inscription, concerns itself with the burial of a cousin of a magistrate, one Maglos; while the third added to the name of the deceased the valuable fact that Justinus was the consul that year. As Justinus was consul in the year 540, the actual year of this burial is known.

All the many simple memorial stones listed by Nash-Williams possessed features that enabled them to be positively identified as Christian. Two, as has been seen, bore the Chi-Rho symbol, many others had crosses of varying types, and a great many carried inscriptions which often gave details of the dead person's father or indicated some other relationship. In making a selection of memorial stones to be visited, as fair a geographical spread as possible has been attempted.

Four stones out of a possible eleven have been selected in the historian's happy hunting ground of Anglesey, of which the first will be found in the chancel of the church at Penrhos Llugwy (481 859), set on high ground to the south of a minor road which branches off the A5025, little more than a mile (1.6 km) north of Llanallgo in the east of the island. The church is locked, but fortunately the chancel glass is clear so that the inscription, which is on the south wall, can be seen through the north window, even the *HIC IACIT* being clearly visible. It is thought to date from the middle of the sixth century and commemorates the death of a Christian Irish chief. This is one of several Irish memorial stones in Anglesey belonging to this period; their surviving relatives were soon to be driven south out of the island by the incoming Christian Celts from Strathclyde, who established themselves at Aberffraw in western Anglesey.

After leaving Penrhos Llugwy the motorist or cyclist will find himself on course for the second memorial stone, if he makes for Llannerch-y-medd in the centre of the island, where he should get on to the B5112, which 7 miles (11.25 km) further on in a south-westerly direction becomes the A4080 when the road crosses the A5. Two miles (3.2 km) further south, still on this road, a lookout should be kept for a single-storey house on the right-hand side named Maen Hir (*maen*: stone; *hir*: long). Opposite this house, just inside a boundary wall on the other side of the road, is the burial stone, Llanfaelog (356 745). It is marked on the OS Map as Inscribed Stone. The simple inscription *CUNDEUS HIC IACIT* refers to a Christian burial in the late fifth or early sixth century. As the visitor gazes at this stone in this remote place, he should marvel that a Christian was buried here at least a hundred years before Pope Gregory sent Augustine north on his civilizing mission to Kent.

This same road, the A4080, after passing through the village of Llanfaelog, leads in 5 miles (8 km) to Aberffraw itself, where Cunedda made his headquarters when he first came down from Strathclyde. Members of his dynasty, who were to rule Anglesey and Gwynedd for many a century, were buried in a royal burial ground 2 miles (3.2 km) to the east where the village of Llangadwaladr now stands. One of these royal memorials survives, having been moved from the churchyard into the village church, where it is now built into the north wall, providing posterity with the most remarkable of all early Christian memorial stones in the whole of Britain. The church (383 693) is always locked but the key may be obtained locally, details in the church porch. The stone on which is also carved a Christian cross, bears this inscription: *CATAMANUS REX SAPIENTISIMUS OPINIATISIMUS OMNIUM REGUM.* (Catamanus wisest and most famous of all kings). Catamanus, which is the Latinised form of Cadfan, was a direct descendant of Cunedda. The memorial was put up in 625 by his grandson, Cadwaladr, who was to give his name to the village and his patronage to the church.

The last of the memorial stones to be visited in Anglesey is in the south-eastern corner of the island, Llansadwrn (555 759), which is north of Menai Bridge and west of Beaumaris. The key to this rather isolated church used to be available from the farmhouse, which is the nearest building to the church. The stone, which was dug up in the churchyard and is now on the north side of the church, is the oldest one in Anglesey, dating from about 530; it commemorates Sadwrn, who was the brother of Illtud himself. The inscription reads: *SATURNINUS SE(PULTUS) (I) ACIT ET SUA SA(NCTA) CONIU(N)X. PA(X) VOBISCUM SIT.* (Saturninus (which is the Latin form of Sadwrn), and his saintly wife lie buried here. Peace be with you both.)

Moving across the Menai Strait to the mainland of northern Wales, the next area to be explored is Llŷn, which furnishes four differing types of early Christian memorial stones. First to the resort of Abersoch, on the south coast, 2 miles (3.2 km) north-west of which is the village of Llangian (295 289), whose churchyard contains a remarkable memorial stone, remarkable in that it bears the first reference to a doctor in the history of the Principality. Tradition assigns the first church here to the sixth century, to the early years of which Nash-Williams also ascribes the stone. It is to be found, probably with some difficulty, in the south side of the churchyard, quite near the south door of the church. Thirty years ago it was reported that the top of the stone had been adapted to form a sundial. This top has now been removed but three holes are still visible in the stone through which the dial was formerly secured. The inscription, which is on the eastern side of the stone, reads *MELI MEDICI FILI MARTINI IACIT.* (Dr. Melius, son of Martin, lies here.) Patience is required to read the inscription nowadays; in a poor light visitors could be forgiven for thinking that they were looking at a plain stone slab! Time is certainly taking its toll of a unique inscription.

Llangwnnadl Church, which is the next place to be looked at, lies about 8 miles (12.8 km) north-west of Llangian across the peninsula, and quite near the north coast. In very early days the little wooden church here provided a welcome resting place for pilgrims on their way from Clynnog Fawr to Bardsey Island. The church is dedicated to Gwynhoedl, who flourished about 600, having been trained at the famous monastery at Bangor-on-Dee. When the present church, a splendid three-aisled building, was being renovated in 1940, an early burial stone was uncovered when the plaster was removed from the south wall. This stone, which some think marked the burial place of the patron saint of the church, carries no inscription but has incised on it a ringed cross, that is a cross within a circle. Faint

Llangadwaladr's inscribed stone

traces of the original red paint on the cross are still visible.

Further evidence of early Christian activity in the peninsula is provided by the church and churchyard at Llanaelhaearn, a large village situated under the brooding presence of Tre'r Ceiri, where people of the Iron Age had settled many centuries previously. The village is on the B4417, about 6 miles (9.6 km) north-east of Nefyn and about the same distance north of Pwllheli. The church is locked but, when last visited, the key was obtainable from No. 6, a house just opposite the church. A late fifth- or early sixth-century inscribed stone, which was dug up in a field near the church, fittingly known as Gardd-y-Sant (*gardd*: garden; *sant*: saint) was taken into the church and set into the west wall. Its Latin inscription, *ALIORTUS ELMETIACO HIC IACET*, informs the reader that the dead man belonged to a far distant Celtic province, Elmet, in what is now eastern Yorkshire. Whether Aliortus died on a visit or in retirement in the district is a matter of surmise. A curiosity about the inscription is the grammatically correct spelling of *IACET*. Just inside the churchyard gate, on the right-hand side, is a second stone, probably still in its original position; the brief surviving inscription indicates that the dead man's name was probably Melitus.

Llystyn Gwyn (482 455) is for the connoisseur rather than for the photographer. Seven miles (11.25 km) along the busy A487, which runs from Porthmadog to Caernarfon, there is a small lay-by on the left-hand side of the road. Park the car here and look eastwards, where half a mile (0.8 km) up a steep farm track is a hill farm, Llystyn Gwyn. In the farmyard is a sixth-century memorial stone with Ogham script along the edge and Latin on its face. Nash-Williams noted that it marked the grave of Icorix, the son of Potentinus. Today the Latin is well-nigh indecipherable, though the Ogham has more successfully withstood the onslaught of the weather. The stone itself is clearly identifiable, as it has been properly built into the wall of the farmyard under a lintel of blue slate. One can but muse upon what sort of a man this Icorix was, and how he came to be commemorated on this bleak and windswept hill.

By way of contrast, the next stone to be tracked down is secure in the busy church of St Mary at Llanrhos (793 803), a suburb of Llandudno. This stone is clearly treasured as it has been excellently mounted. The priest, Sanctinus, we are told, rests here in peace. The date of the burial was probably early in the sixth century. An accompanying brass plate states the known facts:

> This stone stood from time immemorial at Tyddyn Holland, a cottage between Bodafon and Little Orme's Head, about 2,187 yards in a straight line from this church and was removed to this place AD 1908.

It is possible that the key to the church may be obtained from the vicarage, which is down the road in the direction of Llandudno.

Last of the stones to be looked at in northern Wales is in the church at Whitford, between Prestatyn and Holywell (147 782). Here at the west end of the nave is a sixth-century stone which originally stood in Plas-yn-Rhos farm, near Caerwys. The inscription runs thus. *HIC IACIT MULIER BONA NOBILIS.* (Here lies Bona, the wife of Nobilis.)

Two beautiful Celtic stone crosses: 1. Carew, (Pembrokeshire); 2. Maen Achwyfan (Flintshire)

Two places are recommended for visits in mid Wales before the richly rewarding area south and west of Brecon is reached. The first of these is Llanerfyl (035 096) a village in Powys, on the Welshpool (*Y Trallwng*) to Dolgellau road beyond Llanfair Caereinion. Here in a round churchyard high above the road is an immense and ancient yew tree, beneath whose sprawling branches a very early Christian tombstone was discovered, belonging to the late fifth or early sixth century. This stone, which is today housed inside the church at the back of the nave, commemorates the death of a 13-year old girl, Rustece, daughter of one, Paterninus. The accompanying words *IN PACE*, which first appeared on memorial inscriptions in the fourth century, indicate that Rustece was a Christian.

The other place in central Wales is the parish church of Llanafan Fawr in Powys (969 558), situated on the B4358, south-west of Newbridge-on-Wye. The church itself, the key to which may be obtained from the Red Lion Inn opposite, was rebuilt 100 years ago, when it was greatly reduced in size. It stands in an immense round churchyard, the north side of which has received no burials. The site, probably a prehistoric one, the church itself being built on top of a mound which could well have been a round barrow. The church is of special interest to prehistorians as the restored porch contains three unusual stones mortared into its east wall: one of which is spiral, inviting comparison with the spirally-decorated stones at Barclodiad y Gawres in Anglesey. Evidence of early Christian activity here, apart from the tradition that St Afan the patron saint is buried in the churchyard, is provided by a broken memorial stone, now lying on its side on the floor of the chancel. Although it bears no inscription, there is incised on it a ringed cross, which is thought to suggest the seventh century.

The district around Brecon is rich in early Christian survivals. In the triangle contained by the A470, the A40 and the A479, south-east of Brecon, there is evidence of early Christian burial on three sites. At the side of the road at Scethrog a sixth-century stone was discovered, dedicated to Nennius, son of Victorinus. This is now in the safekeeping of the museum in Brecon. The other sites in this triangle are the parish churches of Llangors and Cwm Du. St Paulinus' Church, Llan-gors (135 275), which lies on the

B4560, just north of the lake of the same name, was heavily restored in the nineteenth century but has custody of three early Christian stones. When last visited, these stones were found to have been moved from their usual place in the church to enable some internal repair work to be carried out. In consequence it was not possible to make a proper inspection of these treasures, the most important and earliest of which is a seventh-century specimen, with a ringed cross carved on its face.

St Michael's Church, Cwm Du (181 238) is a few miles to the south-east, on the A479 road between Talgarth and Abergavenny. This is a fine old church, standing up impressively as befits a Michael dedication, in a very large round churchyard, the periphery of which is marked by more than 25 yew trees. There are two early Christian stones here; one is lodged in the porch adjoining the priest's door, a Latin Cross adorning a late sixth- or early seventh-century pillar stone, while the other has been built into a southern buttress halfway between the south porch and the priest's entrance. This sixth-century memorial slab is inscribed with CATACUS   HIC   IACIT   FILIUS TEGERNACUS; apparently this Catacus stone was found in a field about a mile (1.6 km) from the church.

In the space of 10 miles (16 km) or so westwards of Brecon, on or near the A40, are to be found three churches, all privileged to have within their precincts evidence of early Christian associations. The nearest to Brecon, just 3 miles (4.8 km) to the west of it on the A40, is the church at Llansbyddyd (012 282), which is dedicated to Cadog, the early sixth-century contemporary of Illtud. The present church is basically fourteenth century, much restored in mid-Victorian times, but it stands in a circular churchyard whose boundaries are marked by nine or ten ancient yew trees. On the north side of this churchyard, almost hidden in a group of mostly untended nineteenth-century graves, is a sixth-century memorial stone. Although it bears no inscription to identify the dead, the slab is unusually decorated, having two ringed crosses, linked by a carved 'stem'. The top cross, in addition, has four small crosses surrounding it.

Trallong is rather difficult to find. Continue on the A40 in a westerly direction for about another 1½ miles (2.4

km), then turn right on to a minor road which soon crosses the Usk. Half a mile (0.8 km) beyond the bridge turn left and the hamlet of Trallong lies about a mile (1.6 km) along this narrow country road. The church (965 297), dedicated to St David, was saved from the ravages of time in 1861 when the present building took the place of its crumbling predecessor. In the course of this wholesale restoration a late fifth- or early sixth-century memorial stone was uncovered in a window, where it acted as a lintel. It is now clamped to the south wall of the nave just inside the church door. There is a double inscription, in Latin and in Ogham, commemorating one Cunocennius. The ringed cross at the top of the slab is thought to have been added a century or so after the burial.

From Trallong either return to the A40 by the outward route or continue westwards until a left-hand turning leads once more to the A40. In either case leave the A40 at Sennybridge, turning left on to the A4067. Half a mile (0.8 km) along this road is the village of Defynnog. The church (925 279), dedicated to Cynog, is on the right-hand side, immediately south of a hotel, and just before the road divides. The mostly fourteenth-century church is on the site of a very early foundation, possibly dating back even to the late fifth or early sixth century, to which period belongs the memorial stone, which is now propped up against the west side of the porch. The Latin inscription names the dead man as Rugnatio, the son of Vendonus. Above the inscription are two crosses, one ringed and the upper resembling a St Andrew design. Both these crosses were thought by Nash-Williams to have been added after the original burial.

For the last excursion in Powys a

Maen Llia

considerable diversion will be necessary, which most of those who make the effort will think well worthwhile. From Defynnog take the left-hand fork on to the A4215. After about a mile turn right on to a minor road, finger-posted Heolsenni. Just before the village of that name is reached turn left and after a few hundred yards/metres turn right again, as though going to Ystrafellte. This road takes to the hills, winding upwards via a hairpin bend, less than a mile (1.6 km) past which will be seen, on the left-hand side, not far from the road, a tall stone, Maen Llia. This ancient and interesting stone is worth a brief visit, but it has no known Christian connection. Continue on the mountain road for another 1½ miles (2.4 km), when a gated track branches off on the right. This is the ancient trackway Sarn Helen. Great care will be needed to identify this gated track – an Ordnance Survey map is essential. The track itself is quite passable for a reasonably-sized car and leads after about ¾ mile (1.2 km) to Maen Madog (919 158), a stone nearly 10 feet (3 m) high, which stands a few feet away from the left verge of the track. This impressive memorial has an inscription carved on its south face, which reads *DERVAC FILIUS*

IUST IC IACIT (Dervacius, the son of Justus, lies here) – a silent fifth- or early sixth-century Christian witness, nearly 1,400 feet (427 m) above sea-level looking out on this bleak moorland.

Llanddewibrefi (664 554) is an upland village in Ceredigion, above the Teifi valley, situated on the B4343 that runs from Tregaron to Lampeter. To this place in reverent pilgrimage come those Welshmen who concern themselves with the life of their patron saint, for a strong tradition insists that St David in 519 actually preached on the very mound on which the present church stands. The sight of the church on the mound prompts the thought that earlier men than St David may also have held this place sacred in prehistoric times. Within the circular walls of the churchyard there survives much to remind today's visitors of early Christian occupation of the site. Built (upside down) into the outside wall of the church is a sixth-century stone inscribed in Latin, while another inscribed stone can be seen outside the east end also. In addition there are four other early memorial stones in the churchyard, probably dating from the seventh to the ninth centuries. All in all Llanddewibrefi is a very special place.

Llanddewibrefi

There are so many churches in this part of Wales which possess early inscribed stones that some selection is essential, though very invidious. Llanddewibrefi had, through its association with St David, to be an automatic choice. In the end a geographical factor was allowed to decide the issue. Llanddewibrefi looks down on the river Teifi, which, in the course of its winding passage to the sea, passes through two locations whose parish churches keep a watchful eye on early Christian memorials, Llanfihangel-ar-arth and Llandysul, before rushing on towards the sea at Cardigan. This rather arbitrary choice inevitably eliminates from inspection a number of inscribed stones well worth visiting, amongst which are those on Caldey Island, and in the churches at Cilgerran, Cynwyl Gaeo, Eglwys Gymyn, Llanboidy, Llan-dawg, Llangeler, Llan-saint, Pendine and Silian.

The church at Llanfihangel-ar-arth stands on a mound in a circular churchyard, suggesting an earlier association with matters of life and death in the Bronze Age. The key to the church may be obtained from the Eagle Inn opposite. The inscribed stone, which used to be propped up outside the church, now has its home in the vestry, south of the chancel. It commemorates in Latin, Ulcagnus, the son of Senomaglus, who lived towards the end of the fifth century.

Three miles (4.8 km) downstream is the busy market town of Llandysul, whose church, dedicated to Tysul (reputedly the cousin of St David), was established here in very early times on the bank of the river Teifi. Among the many features of this impressive church is an inscribed stone,

St Dogmael's Church

now inserted in the inside wall of the west tower. It is but a fragment of a larger slab which once served as part of a stile that gave access to the churchyard. What remains of this sixth-century inscription reads, *VELVOR FILIA BROHO*. (Velvoria, the daughter of Brohomaglus, lies here.) Another Christian survival here is an ancient altar that now forms part of the stone altar in the Lady Chapel, which the local church guide rightly refers to as 'one of the most important relics in all Wales'.

Twenty miles (32 km) to the west, the river Teifi is finally swallowed up in the sea at Cardigan. Before moving south down a coast wonderfully rich in historical evidence which illuminates many different chapters of the human story, a brief excursion northwards is recommended, to Penbryn, where at the top of a field not far from the sea is an inscribed stone, 6 feet (1.8 m) high (289 514). It is to be found about ½ mile (0.8 km) south of the church and immediately opposite Dyffryn Bern

Holiday Park. The inscription is interesting: *CORBALENGI IACIT ORDOVS* (the stone of Corbalengus. He lies here, an Ordovician). Though the stone was carved in the late fifth or early sixth century, the mason saw fit to remember that the dead man was a member of the Ordovicians, a Celtic tribe which the Romans thought they had obliterated before the year 100.

Just over a mile (1.6 km) south of Cardigan is the large village of St Dogmaels. Near the very considerable ruins of St Mary's Abbey is the parish church (164 459), whose precincts contain yet another sixth-century inscribed memorial stone; this one, which is between 6 and 7 feet (1.8–2.1 m) high, bears on it inscriptions both in Latin and in Ogham – Commemorated here is Sagranus, the son of Cunotamus. Of added interest is the fact that it was the study of these clearly-inscribed stones at St Dogmaels that enabled scholars in 1848 to unravel the secrets of the Ogham alphabet, whose use does not seem to have survived the sixth century.

Cardigan at the mouth of the Teifi was the most southerly part of the territory ruled over by the successors of Cunedda, who, it has already been stated,

dispossessed Christian Irish immigrants, who had preceded them in settling in Wales. South of Cardigan, however, the Irish felt safe; hence south of the Teifi the greatest concentration of the Irish Ogham script is to be found. About 10 miles (16 km) south-west of Cardigan, according to tradition, an Irish monk called Brynach established himself in a secluded well-wooded area under a hill and built himself a church sometime in the sixth century. Today's church at Nevern (082 401), hidden in a valley and approached through an avenue of yews, is dedicated to him. In the churchyard near the south door and slightly to the east of it stands a splendid fifth- or sixth-century memorial stone, commemorating, both in Latin and in Ogham, Vitalianus Emeretus. Inside the church, on a window sill on the south wall of the nave is another inscribed stone, again in both Latin and Ogham, to the memory of Maglicunus the son of Clutorius. This slab was originally found in the wall of the passage that led to the priests' chamber above the nave. There is a third feature in Nevern, which illustrates the importance of the area in early Christian times; about 130 yards (118 m) up a hill to the west of the church towards

Two early crosses at Nevern

Frongoch is the Pilgrims' Cross, a cross cut into the rock face above a stone recess, where pilgrims knelt in prayer. This hallowed spot is thought to have been a wayside shrine for pilgrims en route from Holywell to St David's.

There are more crosses incised on stones in the Fishguard area further south. At Llanllawer (986 359), about 2 miles (3.2 km) south-east of the town, in the Gwaun valley, a large cross was carved in the sixth century on a gatepost at the entrance to the church, the special reason for which can only be guessed at. Again, at Llanwnda (932 392), 2 miles to the north of Fishguard, east of Strumble Head, several stones with crosses carved on them have been built into the outside walls of the parish church. In the late eighteenth century Fishguard enjoyed a few brief days of fame when 1,200 Frenchmen were prevented from making a successful landing in west Wales.

There is one more stone to be viewed with a cross carved on its face; it is situated (838 306) at the side of the road on the A487, south of Fishguard on the way to St David's, a mile (1.6 km) north-east of the village of Croes-goch. Known as Mesur-y-dorth, it is a vertical slab of stone set into the wall; on it a rough cross has been carved in a circle, which tradition associates with St David, who is reputed to have caused it to be carved to act as a pattern for a large loaf of bread to be conformed to in a period of shortage! It is probably a memorial stone dug up in the neighbourhood, and resembles a similar stone which is ascribed to the seventh century, now propped up against an inside wall of St Non's Chapel.

The last church to be visited is quite difficult to find, although it is little more than 7 miles (11.26 km) east of St David's. It would be as well to look to the heavens for guidance, as the church is near what was the RAF fighter training station at Brawdy (*Breudeth*), now known as Cawdor Barracks, which is currently occupied by the Royal Signals, being the main electronic warfare base of the British Army. There is little sign of life in Brawdy except for the aerodrome and a farm next to the church (858 240), whose churchyard is both circular and very large, and in summer much overgrown with brambles. In the porch are three memorial stones, two of which are horizontal and the other vertical. This vertical stone has a Latin inscription, as does the smaller of the horizontal ones; the other one has a message in Ogham. Two of these gravestones have holes in them, suggesting that at some time in their long history they may have been used as gateposts. Inside the church there is a fourth memorial stone, with an incomplete inscription in Latin. All in all visiting Brawdy is rather like finding unexpected signs of life on a desert island!

While most early Christian inscribed memorial stones in Wales are still to be found in churches and churchyards, some of them have been removed to museums for safe custody, especially those that have been discovered at the side of

Clynnog Fawr

the road, or dug up by the plough. Both Swansea Museum and Margam Abbey Museum of Stones have on exhibition stones well worth viewing, but the major collections are to be seen in the museums at Brecon, Carmarthen (*Caerfyrddin*) and Cardiff, a visit to Brecon being a necessary complement to visits to those sites in south Powys already described.

Field and farm, as well as churchyard, have yielded up six inscribed stones for which the new museum at Carmarthen, formerly the Bishop's Palace, has provided an ideal setting. Lastly a leisurely visit to the National Museum of Wales in Cardiff is highly desirable by way of rounding off a study of these early Christian stones. As befits a national museum, it contains inscribed stones from all over the country, from Gwynedd to Pembrokeshire and Glamorgan, all set out to the best possible advantage.

Earlier, the importance of wells in the early days of the Christian church in Wales was discussed, surviving wells near St David's and near Clynnog Fawr in Llŷn in particular showing a close connection with St David and St Beuno respectively. Again and again Christian missionaries, who were forced to settle near a suitable supply of water, tended thereafter to bless these wells thus sanctified in Wales in the fifth, sixth and seventh centuries, some of which had already been in use in pagan times. Of the many wells, a few well-known examples that are still clearly recognisable as wells will here be described.

Many of these old wells are no longer shown even on Ordnance Survey maps, though where they are marked in gothic type, indicating their antiquity, an investigation is well worthwhile. In the nineteenth and even in the early years of the twentieth centuries, parish records frequently referred to ceremonies taking place at church wells on special occasions, such as Easter Monday, Whit Sunday and more particularly on Trinity Sunday. Groups of boys and girls and young adults gathered at the church and together went to the appropriate wells. Various small

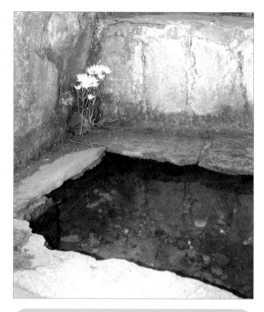

Seiriol's well at Penmon

offerings were thrown into the water, of which the commonest were bent pins, before a ceremonial eating of cakes and drinking of sweetened water gave way to general dancing and merry-making. In the course of time, as the emphasis on enjoyment became ever stronger, the expedition came to resemble a Sunday School treat, whereas in fact it was the

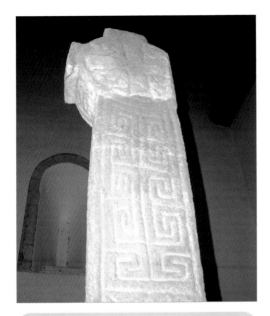

An early Celtic cross at Penmon

Of the four wells to be visited, two are in the north and two in the south. The first one is at Penmon, in the south-east corner of Anglesey, where Cynlas founded the first Christian church in the sixth century, appointing his brother Seiriol to be in charge. This first Christian church was destroyed by the Vikings in the tenth century, to be followed by the erection of the Norman church of today, less than a hundred yards/metres north-east of which is St Seiriol's well (632 808). The small rectangular room over the well was probably put up in the eighteenth century. Underneath it is the well as Seiriol would have known it. Next to the well are the foundations of a hut, which in all probability was St Seiriol's cell. Here the missionary lived and followed his calling, baptising in the well those he won over to Christianity. Just off the coast at this point is Puffin Island, which the Welsh call *Ynys Seiriol*, Seiriol's Island; on this little island are the remains of a monastery which in folk-memory is associated with St Seiriol. In another section of this book a return visit will be made to Penmon in order to relate Penmon's reaction to Viking ruthlessness.

The most famous well in Wales is

spiritual descendant of the ancient pilgrimage that took place from church to well on the patronal day. This patronal day custom too, be it remembered, was the successor in turn of the well-worship that was widespread in pre-Christian times when it was thought prudent to placate with suitable gifts the deities who were believed to live in wells.

undoubtedly the one at Holywell, near the Dee estuary. No further details need here be given about the legend that associated it with St Beuno and his courageous niece Winifrede, whom he saved for higher things! Suffice to say that St Winifrede's Well, whether in origin pagan or Christian, has down the centuries attracted pilgrims who came there to take advantage of the water's healing powers. Beneath today's ornate church and well chamber is St Winifrede's Well, in front of which is a bath where the afflicted seek relief from their ailments. Long before the Norman church was erected a cult had developed, partly as a result of the legend, and partly as a consequence of its growing reputation as a restorer of health. Its fame spread far and wide, and over the years three kings of England have gone there on pilgrimage, William the Conqueror, Edward I and James II. The Catholic church, in whose safekeeping the church and the well reside, treats the well as a Welsh Lourdes. As late as in the middle of the nineteenth century local records reported that large numbers of visitors came to the well every year. The immense flow of water was trapped early in the twentieth century by a local magnate, who operated a lead mine, but though the supply of water has in consequence been much reduced, its curative properties remain popular.

By way of a complete contrast the third well lies hidden in remote and hilly country, far beyond the reach of all but the totally committed, for whom an appropriate reward will be forthcoming when finally they see Partrishow. The approach, preferably in a small car, is via the A465 Hereford to Abergavenny road. At Llanfihangel Crucornau turn north into the Honddu valley as though going to Llanthony Abbey; after 1½ miles (2.4 km) turn left at a telephone kiosk and continue on the narrow road for 2 miles (3.2 km) until a crossroads is reached. The right-hand turning is labelled Partrishow but is better ignored as it involves half a mile (0.8 km) of hard walking later on. Go on straight across the bridge and keep on this road to a T-junction, where the road to the right after a mile (1.6 km) will lead to a really steep hill, at the foot of which is a flat place on the left-hand side by a stream. Park here and cross the road to the well. This is the Holy Well of Issui, where the history of Partrishow began.

According to tradition, Issui, a sixth-century Christian missionary, lived in a cell close to this well (279 224); from these modest headquarters he moved around the district, preaching, teaching and above all healing, until one day a traveller, whom he had befriended, saw fit to murder him. Thereafter it was believed that the healing powers of Issui were transferred to his well, to which from then on pilgrimages were frequently made. This went on for many years until early in the eleventh century one of the pilgrims who had been smitten with leprosy had the good fortune to be cured by the waters of the well. In his gratitude he provided enough money for a church to be built up the hill above the well. This church, now called Partrishow, was at first known as Merthyr Issui, the Martyred Issui. A further reward will await today's visitor, who climb up the hill to the church, which is about 100 yards/metres above the well. They will find that magic has somehow survived at Partrishow.

The last well to be visited is near Tryleg, once a prosperous market town high up above the Wye valley, south of Monmouth in Gwent. Now called the Virtuous Well, because its chalybeate waters are believed to have cured many afflictions, it was in earlier times known as St Anne's Well. An early tradition asserted that there were at one time no fewer than nine wells in the neighbourhood, all of which were credited with curing different complaints.

External Threats

The Saxon and Viking Menace: Vacuum in Wales

Historians date the lapse of Roman power in Britain from 410. In Wales, however, the Roman writ ceased some years earlier, probably in 383, when the Emperor, the Spanish-born Christian soldier Magnus Maximus led away his Roman troops from Wales to undertake important new duties in distant Gaul.

Magnus Maximus became known as Macsen Wledig when he married the Welsh Elen in Caernarfon. This Welsh wife was the same Elen whose name survives in the old Roman road, Sarn Elen, which still runs in a north-south direction here and there in Wales today. She has sometimes been confused with the more famous Helen who was credited with having found the true cross when on a pilgrimage to Jerusalem; this Helen's even more famous son, the Emperor Constantine, has also sometimes been confused with the Welsh Elen's husband, the Emperor Magnus Maximus, despite the fact that Constantine ruled much earlier in the fourth century than the usurping Magnus Maximus.

Thereafter, for a while there was no central authority in Wales, though at least in all probability it was spared the bitter turmoil that prevailed in areas further east in southern Britain after the withdrawal of the Roman legions. The invaluable evidence to be gathered from surviving inscribed Christian memorial stones in Wales in the fifth and sixth centuries suggests a society in which there was room not only for priests and missionaries, but also for local government officers, and even, as is provided by an inscription in a churchyard in Llŷn, for a doctor. However, in southern parts of Wales the quarrels between evenly-matched, insecurely-organised and independent Celtic tribes were of such a nature that the clock was put back once the strong arm of Roman protection was lost. Another important factor operating in the south was the absence of the custom of primogeniture; estates became smaller as time went on and the laws of inheritance weakened the existing structure of local society. Thus the emergence of stronger units was thwarted, units which might have at least been able to assume some regional authority and exercise a measure of control over warring tribesmen.

Great Orme
(Penygogarth)
Maen Achwyfan
Chester
Aberffraw
Penmon Cross
Eliseg's Pillar
Bangor-on-Dee
Bardsey
Shrewsbury
Knighton
Hereford
Offa's Dyke
Nevern Cross
Fishguard
Dinefwr Castle
Whitland
Carew Cross
Tenby
Penally Cross
Lydstep
Swansea
(Sveins-ey)
SKOKHOLM
SKOMER

→ VIKING - - → NORTHUMBRIAN •••• MERCIAN

married Hengist's daughter, played no proven part in Welsh events, despite the prominence assigned to him in folklore in connection with strange and magic happenings in the Gwynant valley on Dinas Emrys, to which hill he possibly withdrew when the pressures of life elsewhere became too great for him to bear.

This same district around Snowdon is much concerned, too, with Arthurian legend; to the security of this mountainous area the wounded hero was carried, according to the legend, when his life was ebbing away. Much romantic nonsense crystallised around Arthur's name, more especially in the twelfth century, when Geoffrey of Monmouth embroidered and embellished the spoken tradition. Arthur seems to have been an outstanding Celtic leader in the first half of the sixth century, half a century after Vortigern had passed from the scene. To Arthur is given the credit for gaining a significant victory against the Saxons at Mount Badon in 516, the battle, Gildas assures his readers, having been fought on the very day of Gildas' birth, but where exactly it took place no-one seems to know.

In the course of this fifth century, when Wales for the most part lived a separate life untouched by the troubles that developed further east in Britain, early Saxon infiltration intensified, especially when the Anglo-Saxon leaders, Hengist and Horsa, were invited to come to Britain by the Celtic leader Vortigern to help him defend his territories against Pictish assaults from the north. Vortigern, whose headquarters were probably in east Wales, and who, according to legend,

The coming of Cunedda

At about this time, when Wales was thus being cushioned from Saxon pressure, a new external threat developed in the north of the country, which began to fill the vacuum brought about by the retreat of Roman soldiers from Wales. Early in the fifth century Cunedda, a Romanised Celt, who was probably also a Christian, led his tribe of Votadini down from Strathclyde. He managed to establish a foothold in the west of Anglesey, where from his headquarters at Aberffraw he began to drive out the Irish immigrants from the island. His grandson Cadwallon completed the expulsion of the Irish from Anglesey when he defeated them in a battle fought near Trefdraeth in about 500. Cadwallon's son, Maelgwn Gwynedd, went a step further, consolidating the political power of the family by centralising the government of northern Wales and ruling it from Aberffraw. In the process he gave his name Gwynedd to the territory on the mainland that he had conquered. As the sixth century wore on, Cunedda's successors went from strength to strength until they ruled a domain that stretched from Anglesey in the north to the mouth of the Teifi at Cardigan in the south.

Northumbrian invasion

Something has already been said about the historic and highly significant meeting that took place at Aust at the beginning of the seventh century, the effects of which were to widen the gap that already existed between the two branches of the Christian church in Britain. Sir Frank Stenton, however, an outstanding authority on Anglo-Saxon England, sounded a note of caution:

> An anecdote never tells the whole truth about a complicated issue and there were many reasons besides Augustine's possible failure in courtesy for a breach between the Roman mission and the British church.

Our knowledge of what happened in Britain in this seventh century suffers from overmuch reliance on the narratives of Bede, the only seventh-century chronicler of events, and himself a Saxon with a thorough dislike of all things Celtic. The basic facts, however, are agreed. In the north-east Northumbria had begun to coalesce and to emerge as a force to be reckoned with. Under the leadership of Aethelfrith, their first able king, the boundaries of Northumbria were extended both northwards and to the west and south-west. Between 613 and 616 he attacked the Celts, whom we may now reasonably call the Welsh, on ground of his own choosing some miles to the south of Chester. Indeed it was from Aethelfrith's victory in this Battle of Chester that his fame as a successful leader was derived. The actual site of the battle was near the modern village of Bangor-on-Dee, the home of the great Celtic Christian monastery from whose much-respected precincts had gone forth those Christian emissaries who had done verbal battle with Augustine in the previous decade.

Tradition has it that before the fighting began, a very large band of monks came out from the nearby monastery in order to pray for those who were about to defend themselves against the invading Aethelfrith and his men; the Northumbrian king, knowingly or otherwise, proceeded to implement the terrible threat that Augustine had uttered at Aust. Aethelfrith slaughtered the monks to a man. The Welsh army, under the command of the son of the King of Powys, fared little better than the monks had done. The victorious Northumbrians,

according to Giraldus Cambrensis, chose to celebrate by destroying Chester, but developments elsewhere prevented Aethelfrith from following up his military success with territorial conquest. Nevertheless, by this serious defeat the Welsh became geographically and politically isolated from their fellow Celts in Cumbria and Strathclyde.

Aethelfrith was succeeded as King of Northumbria by Edwin, who took upon himself the responsibility of continuing Northumbrian domination over the Celts by bringing about the complete destruction of the old northern kingdom of Elmet. It was this Edwin who managed to drive the final wedge between the Celts in the west and their fellows in the north. The tide eventually turned against him, however, when, after an attempt to capture parts of northern Wales failed, he was thrown back and even pursued into his own territories by Cadwallon, scion of the house of Cunedda. In alliance with Northumbria's enemy Mercia, Cadwallon defeated and killed Edwin in 632. As things were to turn out this success of Cadwallon proved an illusion; his death in battle the following year near Hexham marked the end of the very last attempt on the part of the western Celts to win back any of the lands in the east which their forebears had formerly inhabited.

By the year 650 the Welsh seem to have accepted the geographical boundaries of contemporary Wales as the limit of their homeland for the foreseeable future. The resulting isolation, which was to continue for about a hundred years, was rendered the more necessary by the stark fact that the men of Mercia (the Mercian-Welsh alliance having proved to be of very short duration) now firmly controlled Herefordshire and Shropshire. From the middle of the seventh to the middle of the eighth century the Welsh turned in upon themselves; consciously or unconsciously, in those years of separation they went on the defensive. They became introspective, as they developed their own language, their own culture, their own institutions, their own self-consciousness.

The centre of government and administration was at Aberffraw, the stronghold established earlier in the west of Anglesey by Cunedda, and faithfully handed down to his successors. In the nearby settlement of Llangadwaladr may still be seen in the parish church historical evidence of events of the early seventh century. In the chancel stands the so-called Catamanus Stone, which was erected to the memory of Cadfan, who died in 625. As well as being a famous king, as the inscription asserted, he was also a famous father as his son was none other than that Cadwallon, who had encompassed the defeat of Edwin of Northumbria.

Mercian aggression

The years of introspection were savagely swept away by the aggressive intentions of the Anglo-Saxons of Mercia; it was in the eighth century that two rulers of Mercia, first Aethelbald and then Offa, fortified their western frontiers with the Welsh. The earlier of the two defence systems, Wat's Dyke, was erected to secure the northern end of Mercia's boundary with Wales, its builders presumably taking advantage of the Roman road system, based on Chester, in order to bring up supplies for the vital work of construction. Here, near Basingwerk on the Dee estuary, there is still impressive evidence of the

1. Offa's Dyke near Clun; 2. The Dee bridge, Bangor-on-Dee; 3. The two hills of Deganwy – the site of one of the castles of Gwynedd

first man-made boundary between the Saxons and the Welsh.

Offa ruled Mercia from 757 to 796. Though his reign was for the most part a very turbulent one, it seems likely that the great earthwork associated with his name was thrown up in a period of relative peace, probably between 784 and 795, when it is known that an uneasy peace prevailed along the frontier. Offa's Dyke, which marked a more or less continuous barrier from the Severn valley in the south to the estuary of the Dee in the north, not only spelt out to the Welsh, 'thus far and no further', but at the same time signified a tacit Mercian acceptance of the Welsh right to rule themselves. It may be seen as positive proof of the sterling qualities of leadership shown by the Welsh, more particularly by the princes of Powys. To thoughtful observers, Offa's Dyke and the surviving portions of Wat's Dyke provide eloquent twentieth-century witness of those troubled years. In addition attention must be drawn to what is probably the most famous memorial in the whole of Wales, Eliseg's Pillar, which stands in a field near *Valle Crucis* Abbey to the north of Llangollen.

The respite in Mercian-Welsh warfare came to an abrupt end in 796, when Offa once again, though for the last time, took the offensive. This attack was followed by a number of others, mounted by his successors in the early years of the ninth century. In 816 Cenwulf invaded the north and managed to get as far as Snowdonia; two years later he turned his attention to Dyfed in the south. When in 821 he died at Basingwerk, he was on the eve of launching yet another campaign against the Welsh. The very next year the new King of Mercia, Ceowulf, the brother of Cenwulf, captured Deganwy before turning south and overrunning Powys. These bitter incursions between 816 and 822 that seemed to represent a new phase in the Mercian attempt to impose its authority over Wales, in fact came to an unexpected end when the Mercians found themselves threatened by a new and formidable enemy from the east, the Vikings. Thereafter, the kingdom of Mercia quite swiftly fell into a decline as the Viking power gathered strength, to the immediate discomfiture of all Saxons and Welshmen alike.

The arrival of the Vikings

These new disturbers of the peace came

from the northern lands. Northmen or Norsemen, Vikings or Danes, whatever name was given to them, they showed themselves to be restless travellers and ruthless fighters. Those who concentrated on attacks from the sea proved themselves such skilful navigators that their expeditions took them to Spain and to Italy, to Iceland and to Russia, to France and to various part of the British Isles. When Charlemagne, who had established in western Europe an empire based on Christian law and order died in 814, his dominions soon crumbled. The men from the north saw their chance and took it. Everywhere they went, their impact was immense; nowhere was it stronger than in Ireland, where an Irish golden age suddenly collapsed in 853, when the Vikings made themselves lords of the island. Their overlordship there was to last for a century and a half and, while it lasted, Wales was made to feel the full blast of Viking attacks, which were mounted from Irish bases.

The very year of this Irish disaster saw the first Viking raid on Anglesey; thereafter the Vikings harried the coast of Wales, north and south, on and off for the 150 years of their Irish occupation. Anglesey itself was invaded on no fewer than seven occasions, the last being in 987. The last of all the Viking incursions into Wales was made in 999, when St David's was devastated, and its bishop murdered. Monasteries and churches were looted and laid waste in those widespread raids, in the course of which a number of Viking trading stations were established along the coast of Wales. Many a place name on Welsh coast and island bears witness to those terrible times. Tenby, Bardsey, the Great Orme, Fishguard, Lydstep, Skokholm and Skomer all speak of their Viking past.

Rhodri Mawr

It was in this tragic period of Welsh history, when the Vikings were attacking from the sea that her south-eastern neighbours, Wessex, were being similarly threatened by other would-be conquerors from the north, the Danes. Just as the dire emergency produced the right leader in Wessex in the person of Alfred the Great, so too in Wales it threw up the mighty Rhodri Mawr, Rhodri the Great. During the first half of the ninth century the course of Welsh history changed direction as the ruling house of Gwynedd set about trying to unify the country, the process seeming to start with Merfyn Frych, the King of Gwynedd, seeking a dynastic marriage. In this, the generation before the Viking threat developed, the well-being of Wales was still being menaced by repeated Mercian thrusts. In order to strengthen Welsh resistance to these attacks, most of which were directed at Powys, Merfyn married Nest, the sister of Powys' resourceful king, Cyngen, and thereby secured an immediate and valuable ally.

When Merfyn died in 844, he was able to bequeath to his son Rhodri both Gwynedd and Powys; to this inheritance Rhodri later added other parts of central and south Wales, with the result that in the course of his thirty-four years' reign he became master of all north and central Wales and a very large part of southern Wales too. Like his father before him, he had made a politically wise marriage when he joined forces with Angharad, the sister of the last King of Cardigan, who in his lifetime had taken over Carmarthen, forming out of the two areas the new kingdom of Seisyllwg.

Thus strengthened at home, Rhodri felt strong enough to face up to the daunting task of trying to hold at bay the Vikings, whose first main target was Anglesey, where in 854 he defeated and killed the Viking leader, Gorm. The respite gained was short-lived, however; nevertheless, while throughout his reign he was plagued by repeated Viking attacks, which he could do nothing to prevent, he at least made sure that these raids could not be followed up by territorial conquest and settlement. On a hill outside Llandeilo, in the Tywi valley in Carmarthenshire, stands the castle of Dinefwr. Here in 876, two years before he died, Rhodri made the necessary arrangements for the future government of Wales after his death. In order to give Wales the unity which he believed she desperately needed he agreed to divide his dominions into three parts, to be inherited by the three strongest of his six sons, one to succeed him in the north, another in the centre and the third in the south.

Not all the rulers who have acquired the designation of 'Great' have really merited the honour; in the case of Rhodri it is perhaps easier than usual to justify the accompanying 'Mawr'. His achievement in dealing so firmly with the enemy at the gate was simple and perhaps negative, but he did at least reduce the Viking menace to manageable proportions, while his court achieved the reputation of being a civilised place where foreigners were free to come and go and where they could speak their own tongues and be understood. Rhodri certainly showed real foresight in planning for future Welsh unity and although those who came after him failed to unify their country, he had provided them with a dynasty which was to rule Wales, both north and south, for many a long year.

By way of footnote it should be added that the young Saxon Alfred, who was also to be known as the Great, had by this time become the King of Wessex, and it is perhaps significant that a year or two after Rhodri's death in 878 his son, Anarawd, who had inherited Gwynedd, saw fit to pay allegiance to Alfred, becoming the first Welshman ever to visit a Saxon court. It has to be borne in mind, however, that towards the end of the ninth century the Viking menace had become so fearsome throughout Western Europe that Alfred's success in dealing with the Danes had caused him to be venerated as the great Christian champion against what were seen as the marauding heathens from the north.

Hywel Dda

Hywel Dda, a grandson of Rhodri Mawr, became ruler of Seisyllwg in 910, at a time when Gwynedd and Powys had once again good reason to fear a renewal of aggression on the part of Mercia. In 911 Aethelflaeda, the daughter of Alfred the Great and sister of Edward the Elder, the King of Wessex, herself became ruler of Mercia, when her husband Aethelred died. For the following eight years there was real anxiety west of Offa's Dyke as the 'Lady of the Mercians' proceeded to fortify strong points at Runcorn in the north on the invasion route into Gwynedd and at Chirbury on the well-worn way into central Wales. Having thus secured herself, she took the initiative. In 916, as the Anglo-Saxon Chronicle records, she sent her army into Powys; in the course of this aggressive campaign the Mercian army destroyed a Welsh stronghold, which had been built in the middle of Llan-gors lake on an artificially-created island. In the summer of 1988 this was uncovered by underwater archaeologists, who dated its building to about 870. Indeed the new threat implicit in the renewal of Mercian ambitions must have been an important factor in the gradual development of an understanding between the various princes of Wales and Wessex. In addition, it is known that Hywel had in his early years greatly admired the achievements of Alfred the Great, especially his stalwart defence of his lands against the Danes. From about 918 the understanding between Welshmen and the men of Wessex flourished and grew into a special relationship between Hywel and Alfred's son, Edward the Elder, ruler of Wessex from 910 to 925. Edward had earned deep Welsh gratitude for securing the release from the Vikings of the Bishop of Llandaf, who had been carried off in a raid.

Hywel Dda had followed in the footsteps of his famous grandfather and great grandfather by greatly increasing his dominions as a result of making a successful marriage. His wife, Elen, daughter of the King of Pembroke, was to bring her husband all the land south-west of Seisyllwg. Again, when Hywel's cousin, Idwal, the King of Gwynedd, and another grandson of Rhodri, died, Hywel was able, without much effort and without attracting too much attention, to take over both Gwynedd and Powys. Thus Hywel found himself, halfway through his reign, virtual ruler of all Wales, enabling him,

when he went on pilgrimage to Rome in 928, to be thought of as 'the King of all the Welsh'.

Clearly in the reign of Hywel Dda the centre of Welsh political gravity moved for the first time since the days of Cunedda from the north of the country to the south. At the same time as this geographical shift of power occurred there came an equally significant shift in policy as the ruler of Wales moved from hostility towards Saxons to co-operation with them. This was no easy change of attitude, nor did it go unchallenged, though the challenge failed. Further evidence of this desire to co-operate with Wessex came in the reign of Athelstan, who succeeded his father Edward on the throne of Wessex in 925. Between then and 928 representatives from Wales met the new King of Wessex in Hereford. At this meeting it became clear that Welshmen even admitted the overlordship of their host, to whom they swore allegiance. The ever-present Viking threat all along the coast of Wales may well have been the determining factor that made the Welsh accept dependence as the

The king, as illustrated in the manuscript of Cyfraith Hywel

price they were prepared to pay to acquire a friend and ally in the emergency; if the understanding did in fact amount to an alliance, then the Welsh were definitely the junior partners. A limited territorial arrangement agreed upon at Hereford concerned the mutual recognition in that area of the river Wye as the boundary between Welsh and Saxon lands.

Protected by this understanding with Wessex, and politically strengthened by it, Hywel ordered the leading Welsh clergy and the most important laymen to meet him at Whitland (*Hendy-gwyn*) in 930. There, a few miles west of Carmarthen, he presented for their earnest consideration and discussion the whole corpus of Welsh law and custom. That they were entrusted with the responsibility of reforming and categorising Welsh laws in this authoritative fashion is positive proof of the powerful position enjoyed by Hywel Dda. This assembly stayed in continual session for 40 days, by which time the all-important decisions had all been taken. For just how much of this codification Hywel was personally responsible cannot now be known for certain, and indeed is sometimes disputed, but his title of 'Dda' dates from this time. Few kings in history have gained the description of 'Good', but Hywel, by his legal work and his persistent attempt to reconcile the religious differences between the Celtic church and Rome, seems to have justified the title, especially when it be remembered that throughout his reign the Vikings posed an ever-present threat. It is worth recalling that, when in after years Edward I of England in 1284 saw fit at Rhuddlan to dictate terms to the Welsh, he thought he was softening the blow by suggesting that he had based his statue only on the laws coded by Hywel. That Hywel Dda was a wise and diplomatic ruler cannot be denied, nor should the years of peace that his policies made possible with his neighbours be underrated. Whether he was good and not just opportunist may be debated, though the laws associated with this name have stood the test of time. Unhappily peace seems to have died with him in 950.

All the efforts of Rhodri Mawr to create Welsh unity by providing the country with a strong dynasty seemed to have failed in the very dark years that followed the death of his grandson Hywel Dda in 950. Hywel for his part had shown one way to peace and unity by co-operating with the Saxons of Wessex; that policy too came to an abrupt end. Even the unifying effect on the Welsh of the constant threat of Viking raids lost its former power, despite the stark fact that half a century more of these ferocious attacks had still to be endured in Wales. The lack of any strong central government showed itself, too, in the excessive power still being enjoyed at the local level by regional princelings. In fact, much of Wales was still a simple society where allegiance to the local family was paramount. All these facts, in addition to the ancient practice of dividing a man's lands between all his sons when he died, together presented Wales with an acute crisis in the middle years of the tenth century, when they suddenly lost the authority of Hywel Dda. This unhappy situation was to become more serious in the years that followed because their adversaries across Offa's Dyke were beginning to take big steps towards achieving their own national unity.

Hence the pattern of events was extremely confused in the second half of the tenth century, as the various descendants of Hywel Dda in different parts of the country indulged in fratricidal contention with each other. In those uncertain times no prince in the north, the centre or the south was strong enough to gain the mastery, which would have enabled him at least for the time being once again to have achieved the unification of Wales, as Rhodri Mawr and Hywel Dda had done in the past. In 986 a glimmer of hope had appeared, but it was to be snuffed out before the end of the century. In 986 Hywel Dda's grandson, Maredudd ab Owain held sway in Gwynedd, Deheubarth and in Dyfed but failed to annex Powys. In 992 he found himself at war with his own nephew, who proceeded to bring in to help him against his uncle an army from Mercia. Maredudd died in 999 and the new century dawned on a Wales more divided than ever.

Gruffudd ap Llywelyn and Saxon Harold

Those very dark hours for Welsh hopes preceded a dawn which lit up the personality of one of the greatest of all Welsh military leaders, Gruffudd ap Llywelyn, whose father Llywelyn ap Seisyll had seized the throne of Gwynedd in 1018, a domain which he was to rule successfully until 1023. His son Gruffudd, according to surviving records, was indolent in his youth, reserving his appearance in public life until 1037 when the King of Gwynedd was cut down by his own men. In the aftermath of this murder, in which Gruffudd himself may well have played a part, he began to stand out as the strong man for whom Wales had been looking. He became King of Gwynedd in 1039, adding Powys to his dominions later in the same year. Before long he had in addition annexed Deheubarth, Morgannwg (modern Glamorgan) and Gwent. In fact, he was thereafter virtually the ruler of all Wales for the rest of his reign.

Gruffudd was a man of immense physical energy and courage: he not only unified Wales (killing many Welshmen in the process) but took the offensive against the English, making a number of successful forays across Offa's Dyke. In 1052 he won a battle near Leominster, following it up three years later by killing 500 English soldiers in the course of capturing Hereford. If the local reports are to be believed, seven cathedral canons stoutly defended the great west door of their church before if was battered down by Gruffudd's men. In 1056 he crossed the dyke once more and again captured Hereford before English reinforcements made him withdraw into the Welsh hills.

Gruffudd's reign roughly coincided with that of the English king Edward the Confessor, whose right-hand man was the Saxon leader, Harold, Earl of Hereford, destined on Edward's death to become the last Saxon king of England. These two giants of men, Gruffudd and Harold, were worthy adversaries; it is perhaps ironical that it was in the reign of one of Wales' strongest and most successful rulers that the hated Saxons came nearest to establishing themselves in Wales. Harold managed to set up Saxon strongholds in Gwent and Powys before setting forth on the attempted invasions of northern Wales in 1062 and 1063. Apparently Harold alone of those who sought to impose their wills upon Wales had given the necessary thought to the choice of suitable tactics. Giraldus Cambrensis, writing 100 years later, spoke highly of his skill as a military planner. He wrote: 'He advanced into Wales on foot, at the head of his lightly-clad infantry, lived on the country and marched up and down and round and about the whole of Wales.' At any rate in 1063 he drove Gruffudd out of his castle at Rhuddlan before destroying it, and then systematically approached the mountainous area around Snowdon, supported by a fleet that stood off the Welsh coast to prevent Gruffudd from receiving supplies from Anglesey. By the end of that tragic summer Gruffudd was on the run; he was to be hunted down and eventually killed by his own Welsh supporters. The despatch of his severed head to Harold marked the end of hostilities and the temporary recognition of the Saxon subjection of northern Wales.

Harold's victory was, however, of short duration: three years later he died in a hail of arrows at Hastings, thereafter leaving Wales exposed to a greater threat even than that ever presented by the Saxons. Gruffudd, despite his humiliating failure in 1063, had by his bravery and leadership stiffened Welsh resolve to resist further invasion. When the Normans, after their rapid conquest and assimilation of England, turned westwards to deal with Wales, they were to be made aware of the strength of Welsh national feeling, which Gruffudd had by his example greatly fostered in his fellow countrymen. The Earls of Hereford, Shrewsbury and Chester, specially created by the Conqueror to extend his authority to the west of Offa's Dyke, were soon to realise the severity of the task assigned to them.

Evidence in Wales Today

Modern wars leave in their wake destruction and war memorials whereas the periodical blood-letting that Saxons and Vikings inflicted on the Welsh left few traces of their activities that were discernible to succeeding generations. Hence surviving evidence of the tumultuous times already described is very thin indeed. The backward-looking enquirer today, who has already been well rewarded by the sight of barrows, long and round, iron-age camps, Roman remains and Christian memorial stones, will now have to be content with a few, though wonderful, crosses, and with Mercian Offa's attempt to bring about a permanent line of demarcation between his domains and those of the Welsh, whose independence was being recognised by the erection of this dyke.

Two miles (3.2 km) north of Llangollen are the spectacular ruins of the Cistercian *Valle Crucis* Abbey, in a field not far from which stands what is probably the most famous memorial in Wales, Eliseg's Pillar (203 445). Originally it was about twice its present height, having in its long history lost both its cross-head and the lower part of its shaft. The cross was sufficiently prominent in the twelfth century for the Cistercian monks who were engaged in building nearby to name their abbey after the cross, which they saw every time they looked up from their work. It was erected early in the ninth century by a king of Powys, Cyngen (who died in Rome in 854), to commemorate the life and martial achievements of his great grandfather, Elise, who was the contemporary of Offa and a worthy opponent of the much-dreaded King of Mercia. The monument was 800 years old when disaster struck; in the course of the civil wars in the seventeenth century, fanatical Puritans hacked at it with venomous fury, seeing in it some reminder of 'Popish practices'. Fortunately for posterity a complete transcript of the inscription on the pillar had been made in the previous century. The pillar lay in ruins until, towards the end of the eighteenth century, the part that survived was put together and re-erected in its present position on a low mound, thought by some to have been the site of a Christian burial in the fifth or early sixth century.

Eliseg's Pillar must have been one of the first of the free-standing crosses, as there is no record of one being erected before the ninth century. The other crosses that have survived mostly date from the early tenth century or later; of these those in the north are thought to have been carved by Celtic craftsmen who had been forced by Viking raiders to leave their homes in Northumbria and in Ireland before taking refuge in northern Wales. Their crosses are noted for the scenes they portray, both human and animal, whereas those in the south of the country were probably the work of local craftsmen who for the most part concentrated on complicated geometrical patterns.

Three of these southern crosses with similar, though by no means identical, motifs will be described, the first at Penally, south of Tenby, not far from Manorbier Castle in Pembrokeshire. St Teilo, the friend and contemporary of St David, is believed to have been both born and buried in Penally (118 992), in whose churchyard there used to stand a tall and beautifully-carved Celtic cross. Today it

1. *Eliseg's Pillar*; 2. *The church and abbey at Penally*; 3. *Offa's Dyke Centre, Knighton*

adorns the south transept of the church near the remains of another early cross, also brought indoors from the churchyard. This one, which unfortunately has lost its cross, dates from the end of the ninth century, while the other one was probably put up a few years later.

A few miles to the north-west of Penally, Carew Cross (047 037) rises majestically at the side of the A4075, about equidistant between Pembroke and Tenby; behind it loom the spectacular ruins of Carew Castle, one of the most impressive castles in south Wales, but several centuries younger than the cross. Carew Cross, at nearly 14 feet (4.26 m), is one of the tallest Celtic crosses in Wales as well as being one of the most intricately-carved, with complicated patterns on both sides and faces of the shaft. A memorial tablet commemorates one Maredudd, son of Edwin, a Welsh prince who was killed in battle in 1035. It is possible, however, that this commemorative tablet to the prince was added many years after the cross was erected, which could well have been in the ninth century.

A second visit to Nevern Church is necessary in order to wonder at the free-standing cross which dominates the south side of the churchyard. Thought to have been erected in about 1000, the cross is reminiscent of the one just seen at Carew and the one still to be looked at at Whitford (Maen Achwyfan). It is about 13 feet (4 m) high, with the surfaces on all four sides of the shaft and the cross-head covered with interlaced decorations of a geometric type. The inscriptions on both faces of the shaft have so far defeated all attempts at deciphering.

Before leaving the south a short visit is recommended to the church at Llanilltud Fawr, wherein will be found the remains of several crosses, dating from the ninth or early tenth centuries. In addition there is a ninth-century cross with a Latin inscription to Samson, who may have been an abbot in the local monastery.

To see the last two crosses a return has to be made to the north. One is in Anglesey, the other in north-east Wales, not far from the Dee estuary. This latter one may be visited at the same time as St Winifrede's Well in Holywell, as the cross at Whitford (Maen Achwyfan), which is over 11 feet (3.35 m) tall, stands in a corner of a field, a mile (1.6 km) west of the village of Whitfor. Dating from the tenth or the eleventh century, this wheel cross (129 787) is carved on all surfaces, its rich decoration an interesting mixture of Scandinavian and Celtic influences. The passage of the years has unfortunately been unkind to this monument, some of its motifs no longer being recognisable.

The last of a number of visits to Anglesey concerns two crosses at Penmon, which has already been described in connection with St Seiriol's Well. The Vikings, whose raids on Wales from newly-acquired bases in Ireland, bedevilled life in Wales for so many years. They first attacked Anglesey in 844, before returning to ravage Penmon in 971. The well-known but now miscalled Deer Park Cross was erected in about 1000, to take the place of an earlier one, destroyed by the Vikings thirty years previously. This outstanding monument, now in a new position in the nave of the church, consists of a shaft, crowned by a circular head, from which stone arms extend on both sides to complete the cross. The decoration, as in all the Celtic crosses seen, is elaborate and intricate, but this one at Penmon has in addition sculptures of human beings and animals; the Celtic tradition here has been reinforced by Scandinavian and Irish influences. There is another tall cross in the church, believed also to date from about 1000; this one stands in the south transept.

The last area to be recommended in this book is Offa's Dyke, the exploration of which affords satisfaction to historians, walkers and nature-lovers alike. In 1971 the Offa's Dyke Long Distance Footpath came into existence; this path, which links Prestatyn with Chepstow, is 177 miles (285 km) long and incorporates in it 60 good miles (97 km) of surviving and recognisable dyke. The Offa's Dyke Association, which looks after the welfare of the dyke and of those who choose to walk upon it, has its headquarters in Knighton, whose Welsh name proclaims its geographical situation: *Trefyclo* (the town on the dyke). Those who want to get a feel of the dyke without involving themselves in too much exercise can do so both north and south of Knighton, leaving their cars in the town and first paying a visit to the old primary school, under whose roof will be found the hospitable office of the Offa's Dyke Association, an admirable exhibition of life in these Marches in former times, and a Youth Hostel. That the dyke rises to both north and south of Knighton illustrates an important fact, namely that it was not intended to be a barrier to keep the Welsh out of Mercia or the men of Mercia out of Wales, but rather it was an attempt to control the passage of men and goods from Mercia into Wales and from Wales to Mercia. The presence of this and other gaps in the dyke was to ensure the proper regulation of movement in both directions.

One particular central section of the dyke has been selected for a closer view to show the impact that it must have made on the ordering of social life in the Marches – that is, the section between the Kerry Ridgeway, west of Bishop's Castle and Churchtown, further south. This area lies inside the mountainous middle section between Montgomery and Knighton. (The B4386 from Montgomery, eastwards towards Chirbury, crosses the dyke a mile (1.6 km) east of the town at a point where the dyke is still the national frontier.) Those wanting to get the most enjoyment out of exploring the walk about to be described need a car and a considerate driver who will be prepared to drop them at the Kerry Ridgeway (258 896) and pick them up later at Churchtown (263 873). It is suggested that the approach by car should be made from Bishop's Castle, a busy little market town in west Shropshire. Take the ever-narrowing country road due west of the parish church, which is at the bottom of the main street, and continue on it for about 3 miles (4.8 km) until Bishopsmoat is reached, noting in the field on the right a well-preserved Norman motte and bailey. At the intersection of roads take the middle one, labelled Pantglas; another cross-roads is approached after about 1½ miles (2.4 km) at Hazel Bank. One mile (1.6 km) further on is the Kerry Ridgeway, where an Offa's Dyke fingerpost, decorated with an acorn, will be seen on a stile on the left bank. Here the walk begins. The car driver, if wise, will retrace his steps to Bishop's Castle, where he should turn south on to the A488. About 2½ miles (4 km) along this road turn right onto another country road, marked Cefn Einion, from where he should use his Ordnance Survey map or satnav to get to Churchtown for the eventual rendezvous with his passengers.

The walkers, meanwhile, will have climbed up the bank on to the dyke itself, which on the Kerry Ridgeway is 1,300 feet

(396 m) above sea level. The path soon leads over a stile into a waymarked wood at the bottom of which is the little river Unk, which has to be crossed by a wooden plank. Ahead rises the dyke again, which now leads steeply to a narrow road, which crosses it on Edenhope Hill (263 883). When some breath has been regained and the spectacular views absorbed, cross the road and get back on to the dyke which stays on the level for about a third of a mile until it crosses a lane, running at right angles. It then drops down sharply into the next valley at Churchtown, which today consists of a house or two and the parish church of Mainstone, (the hamlet of that name lying a mile further to the east). This church has the distinction of being the only Anglican church in Shropshire not to be mentioned by Pevsner! It is probable that a little community grew up here in early times to satisfy the needs of those who passed that way through the gap in the dyke. Before getting back to the waiting car, cast a glance across the road to where the dyke soon climbs steeply up again and out of sight on to wild and beautiful country to the west of Clun.

Bibliography

D. Berry, *Walks in the Hidden Heart of North Wales*, 2007.

E. G. Bowen, *The Settlements of the Celtic Saints of Wales*.

Giraldus Cambrensis, *Itinerary of Wales*.

C. Houlder, *Wales: An Archaeological Guide*.

Francis Jones, *The Holy Wells of Wales*.

V. E. Nash-Williams, *The Early Christian Monuments of Wales*.

R. E. M. Wheeler, *Prehistoric and Roman Wales*.

A. H. Williams, *An Introduction to the History of Wales*, Vol. I: Prehistoric Times to AD 1063.

By the same author:

Wales Before 1536 – a guide (New edition)
Wales After 1536 – a guide (New edition)
Radnorshire – A Historical Guide
Country Churchyards in Wales

Welsh place names

Abergavenny *Y Fenni*
Anglesey *Ynys Môn*
Bangor-on-Dee *Bangor Is-coed*
Bardsey Island *Ynys Enlli*
Barry *Y Barri*
Beaumaris *Biwmares*
Berriew *Aberriw*
Brecon *Aberhonddu*
Brecon Beacons National Park *Parc Cenedlaethol Bannau Brycheiniog*
Cable Bay *Bae Trecastell*
Caerleon *Caerllion*
Caldey Island *Ynys Bŷr*
Cardiff *Caerdydd*
Cardigan *Aberteifi*
Carmarthen *Caerfyrddin*
Carmarthenshire *Sir Gaerfyrddin*
Chepstow *Cas-gwent*
Conwy valley *Dyffryn Conwy*
Cowbridge *Y Bont-faen*
Denbigh *Dinbych*
Denbigh Moors *Mynydd Hiraethog*
Devil's Bridge *Pontarfynach*
Fishguard *Abergwaun*
Gower *Gŵyr*
Holy Island *Ynys Cybi*
Holyhead *Caergybi*
Holywell *Treffynnon*
Knighton *Trefyclo*
Lampeter *Llanbedr Pont Steffan*
Llandrindod Wells *Llandrindod*
Llandovery *Llanymddyfri*
Llantwit Major *Llanilltud Fawr*
Loughor *Casllwchwr*
Monmouth *Trefynwy*
Monmouthshire *Sir Fynwy*

Montgomery *Trefaldwyn*
Nash Point *Yr As Fach*
Neath *Castell-nedd*
Nevern *Nanhyfer*
New Radnor *Maesyfed*
Newbridge-on-Wye *Pontnewydd-ar-Wy*
Newport *Casnewydd*
Old Radnor *Pencraig*
Partrishow *Patrisio*
Pembrokeshire *Sir Benfro*
Pendine *Pentywyn*
Preseli hills *Mynydd Preseli*
Radnorshire *Sir Faesyfed*
Snowdon *Yr Wyddfa*
Snowdonia *Eryri*
St Asaph *Llanelwy*
St David's *Tyddewi*
St Dogmael's *Llandudoch*
St Lythan's *Llwyneliddon*
Tenby *Dinbych-y-pysgod*
Trecastle *Trecastell*
Valle Crucis Abbey *Abaty Glyn y Groes*
Welshpool *Y Trallwng*
Whitford *Chwitffordd*
Worms Head *Pen Pyrod*
Wrexham *Wrecsam*